Designed Landscape Forum 1

S P A C E M A K E R   P R E S S

Washington, DC

Cambridge, MA

Front cover:
Therapeutic Garden for Children,
Wellesley, MA. Photo: Douglas Reed

Publisher: James G. Trulove
Designer: Sarah Vance
Assistant Designer: Elizabeth Reifeiss
Editors: Gina Crandell, Heidi Landecker
Production Coordinator: Susan McNally
Printer: Palace Press, Hong Kong

ISBN 1-888931-12-4

Contents

**From the Editors
of Spacemaker Press**

This volume marks the first effort by Spacemaker Press to establish a new form of communication for the design professions. Where most publications offer only a selective sampling of design, whether in art, landscape, architecture, or graphic design, this volume constitutes a broad survey of the state of the art of landscape design, in all its permutations, variety, and locales, at the end of the second millennium.

The projects included in these pages were submitted to the Designed Landscape Forum conference in San Francisco in November 1996. But whereas a conference requires a process of sifting and sorting that yields a group of projects for the purpose of presentations, our purpose in compiling this book was to survey the profession as a whole. We are more interested in showing the breadth and variety of the work than in making judgment about its quality. That we leave to readers of this volume.

Because we have tried to graphically portray 255 different projects, we relied largely on the entry forms and project descriptions that accompanied the submittals. We were dismayed to find a number of gaps in the information provided. Surprisingly, some submittals neglected to mention the designer of the project. Others left the name of the firm off the project description, and we had to make deductions (we hope, correctly) based on information provided elsewhere. Still others omitted the locale, size, and distinguishing characteristics of the projects. Many stressed the ideas behind the projects without conveying clearly how those ideas were expressed.

With so many projects to publish, the editors found it impossible to contact every firm to fill these gaps. Instead, we adopted a "triage" system in which we contacted firms to correct the most egregious errors or omissions. Obviously, this system will not satisfy everyone, and if we made mistakes in attribution or characterization of a project, we hope designers and readers will accept our heartfelt apologies. We urge all readers interested in submitting work for the next Designed Landscape Forum to include a detailed project description that incorporates firm name, designer, location, size, and date of the project. (Information can be found on page 215).

The images in this volume convey a comprehensive impression of the art of landscape design, accompanied by analyses by some of the best critics in the Western world in the 1990s. It is a compilation that reveals a great deal about the state of our art. However, as the essay by critic John Beardsley points out, readers should also consider the type of work that is *not* represented in these pages.

Where, for example, in our increasingly global culture are the projects for societies in the developing world? A few are represented here in the form of reclamation and preservation of natural areas in Central and South America. But while designs for institutions and corporations in the Westernized cities of Japan are well-documented, where are the parks, the roads, the restorations of cultural centers in the poorer yet rapidly growing cities of South Asia? Where are the civic, religious, and preservation projects of Africa, with its rich, diverse, and beautiful—albeit different—cultural history of art and design? Where are the landscape designs and urban plans for Bombay, for Zanzibar, for Cairo?

Landscape design and art do have a presence in these regions, but that presence is only barely apparent from the submittals generated by the first Designed Landscape Forum. So, while we have tried to offer a broad survey without bias or selection, even we must admit that this volume's view is presented through the lens of Western culture. But the Designed Landscape Forum 1 is only a beginning. Our goal, through future conferences, symposiums, and publications, is to dramatically broaden that view.
—The Editors

Designed Landscape Forum

In November 1995 a group of landscape designers and artists formed the Designed Landscape Forum. Our purpose was quite simple: For years, many intriguing works of design in the landscape have been proposed and executed internationally. These works, whether identified as art on the land, landscape design, architecture, or environmental design, represent a spectrum of individual, institutional, recreational, developmental, and preservation or reclamation efforts that are culturally ambitious. They may attempt narrative and formalism, range in scale from the intimate to the monumental, and explore various degrees of naturalistic and synthetic delineation. Contemporary design on the land signifies a great breadth of style and cultural expression.

Despite these many projects being conceived and built around the world, the Designed Landscape Forum recognized that there are few opportunities for design-oriented professionals to exchange ideas and review the work of their colleagues in the same or similar fields. Only partial and transitory views are presently available through existing organizations and publications. It was and is the intent of the Designed Landscape Forum to establish an alternative information flow and exchange.

We proposed, through a combination of meetings and conferences, review programs, and publications, to increase dialogue in the various landscape-related professions, extending and promoting a healthy interest in the production of open-space design. We hoped to further consider the specific physical and visual products of our colleagues and to increase visibility and critical discussion. Designers, patrons, artists, historians, journalists, photographers of the designed landscape, and critics were all encouraged to participate in design recognition programs and conferences of colleagues from around the world. From these programs, the Designed Landscape Forum planned to generate an annual or biannual "state of the art" publication.

In November 1996, the first conference on the Designed Landscape was held at the San Francisco Museum of Modern Art. Three hundred artists, architects, landscape architects, urban designers, environmental graphic designers, design teachers, patrons, photographers, and journalists from all over the world met, examined, and discussed the state of landscape art and design at the end of the twentieth century.

Three panels of distinguished designers, artists, critics, and academics reviewed the 255 submittals—which proved to be of considerable interest, quality, and breadth of subject. These panelists—John Beardsley, James Corner, Frederic Christophe Girot, Douglas Hollis, Ricardo Legorreta, Michael Manwaring, Elizabeth K. Meyer, Laurie Olin, Adèle Naudé Santos, Martha Schwartz, and Marc Treib—led the discussion with spirited participation from the floor. Although no awards or prizes were intended, a few projects were incorporated into the panelists' presentations. A second discussion group was held on the following morning at an accompanying gallery pin-up of all the submittals. Following the close of the conference, panelists Elizabeth Meyer, Marc Treib, John Beardsley, and James Corner each contributed essays about the work presented, the state of landscape art and design in the United States and globally, and what the submittals and the conference conveyed about the future of the profession.

For this volume, the DLF publications committee and the editors of Spacemaker Press made several decisions in the interest of broadening and extending the substance of the conference to readers:

1. The editors included images of all 255 submissions.

2. In addition to descriptions and several images of the majority of projects discussed by the panelists, they included descriptions and images of many other submittals.

3. The editors included the essays of the four panelists who represent criticism and academia; they included a brief graphic representation of the work of each of the panelists who represent art and design.

4. To ensure easy comparison for readers, the editors grouped the projects into seven broad categories: gardens, land art, parks, preservation and reclamation, urban design, institutions, and corporations.

In 1998, a second Designed Landscape Forum/Spacemaker Press publication on unbuilt landscapes is planned. A second DLF conference, to be held on the East Coast, is in the early planning stages.

The members of the Designed Landscape Forum and its advisory board wish to extend special thanks to the conference and publication committees, conference participants, and to those who submitted work to the conference.

Board of Directors
Cheryl Barton, President
William Callaway, Financial Officer
Ken Natkin, Secretary
Richard Burns
Stuart Dawson
George Hargreaves
Leah Levy
James Trulove
Peter Walker
Norie Clarke, Forum Director

Advisory Board
May Arbegast
George Baird
Julie Bargmann
Cheryl Barton
John Beardsley
Aaron Betsky
Cathy Deino Blake
Catherine R. Brown
Joe Brown
James Burnett
Pamela Burton
Adele Chatfield-Taylor
Susan Child
James Corner
Stuart Dawson
Boris Dramov
Garrett Eckbo
Phil Enquist
Ken Fieldhouse
Felice Frankel
Adriaan Geuze
Kathryn Gustafson
Richard Haag
Richard Hawkes
Doug Hollis
Walter Hood
John Dixon Hunt
David Ireland
Linda Jewell
Jory Johnson
William Johnson
Mary Margaret Jones
Dan Kiley
Alex Krieger
John Kriken
Ricardo Legorreta
Mia Lehrer
Michael Manwaring
Rodolfo Machado
Elizabeth Meyer
Enric Miralles
Mary Miss
William Morrish
Darrell Morrison
Anna Murch
Laurie Olin
Michael Painter
Thomas Papandrew
Susan Rademacher
Reuben Rainey
Robert Riley
Robert Royston
Adèle Naudé Santos
Yoji Sasaki
Mario Schjetnan
Martha Schwartz
Melanie Simo
Buster Simpson
Ken Smith
Sarah Speare
Elias Torres
Marc Treib
Billie Tsien
Michael Van Valkenburgh
Alan Ward
Ron Wigginton
Tod Williams
John Wong

Conference Committee
George Hargreaves, Chair
Aaron Betsky
Cathy Deino Blake
William Callaway
Jim Grimes
Andrzej Karwacki
Mia Lehrer
James Lord
Kendra Taylor

Publication Committee
Peter Walker, Chair
Julie Bargmann
Cheryl Barton
Richard Burns
Garrett Eckbo
Linda Jewell
Mary Margaret Jones
Leah Levy
James Trulove

**From George Hargreaves
Chair**

As I sit down to write an introduction to what may be one of the more unique documents produced in association with landscape, I am reminded of several meetings in a Bush Street loft in San Francisco, California. At the behest of Pete Walker and Jim Trulove, a loose confederation of interested people began gathering there, seeking to broaden, deepen, and elevate the discourse on landscape. This was the beginning of the Designed Landscape Forum. The Forum took as its mission the exposure of more landscape accompanied by a deeper level of critical dialogue than had been attained through the current media. In doing so, our goal was to give the works of landscape a chance to become a culturally provocative subject for a larger societal audience. This took two forms, the first being the assembly of the professional and academic tribes in San Francisco on November 7-8, 1996, for a real-time discussion of designed landscapes. At the conference, we exhibited the submissions culled from a wide range of designers and artists. These were reviewed in advance by the invited panel, comprising the most penetrating critics of landscape, who led an open forum on designed landscape the following day.

The ensuing conversations between the panel members and the audience as the slides of projects selected for discussion were shown were undoubtedly the most fruitful dynamic of the conference. The following panelist essays in this book (our second strategy for pursuing our larger goal) artfully blend the critical landscape issues identified by the panelists during the conference with the hindsight of thoughtful reflection. I, for one, find an interesting consistency in visions for the future among a remarkable group of writers representing different trajectories of criticism. If theory leads built work, as John Beardsley suggests, do we see in these writings an outline of upcoming landscapes?

Also included in this documentation of the conference are all the submissions. Their variety in context and origin is reflective of the Forum's efforts to cast the broadest of nets to include artists, architects, landscape architects, environmental and graphic designers, photographers, and writers. This scope represents a snapshot of contemporary cultural producers who directly influence the design of the landscape. The many sources of ideological infusion into designed landscape is a fundamental acknowledgment of the Designed Landscape Forum, as is its desire to serve and increase landscape's intellectual audience.

Our first efforts at expanding horizons are now complete. Only time will tell whether they are successful and what other forms and forums may take place in the future.
—George Hargraeves
Chair, Designed Landscape Forum

Postscript: Any conference run on a shoestring must thank its many volunteers who gave their most precious commodity—time.

Anna Amundsen
Martha Folger
Jim Grimes
Chris Guillard
Sandra Harris
Hawley Holmes
Laura Jerrard
Dirk Johnson
Mary Margaret Jones
Rhonda Killian
Sarah Kuehl
Kate Lacouture
Michael Manwaring
Michael Sanchez
Jenni Zell

John Beardsley is a writer, teacher, and exhibition curator who specializes in environmental and public art, garden and landscape history, and folk or "outsider" art. Through his writings, Beardsley has explored how environmental art is affecting the design and symbolic form of public spaces. His book, *Earthworks and Beyond: Contemporary Art in the Landscape*, evolved out of an exhibition for the Hirshhorn Museum in 1977. Subsequent publications and exhibits have examined public environmental art from a variety of perspectives, and his exhibitions featuring black and Hispanic folk art have toured museums throughout the country. His study of environmental art, including the sculptural/architectural creations of self-taught artists and folk artists, is the subject of his most recent book, *Gardens of Revelations*. He has held teaching positions in the landscape architecture departments at the University of Virginia, University of Pennsylvania, and at the Harvard University Graduate School of Design.

James Corner is an associate professor of landscape architecture and regional planning at the University of Pennsylvania Graduate School of Fine Arts. Two current books, *Taking Measures Across the American Landscape* and *The Recovery of Landscape: Contemporary Topics in Landscape Architectural Theory*, are published by Yale University Press and the Architectural Association respectively. Numerous essays have been published in *Landscape Architecture, Landscape Design, Word and Image, AA Files*, and *VIA*. Corner has lectured widely across the United States and Europe, served as visiting professor at the University of Norway, and served as the Daniel Urban Kiley Lecturer at Harvard in 1993. He has practiced professionally in the offices of Robert Fleming and Associates, Wallace Roberts and Todd, and Gillespie and Partners. He was the first recipient of the George Holmes Perkins Award for Distinguished Teaching and Innovation in Methods of Instruction from the Graduate School of Fine Arts at the University of Pennsylvania and was recently appointed the first Jens Jensen Professor in Landscape and Urbanism at the University of Illinois at Chicago School of Architecture.

Frederic Christophe Girot received his master of architecture and landscape architecture from the University of California, Berkeley. He is now practicing landscape architecture in Paris, where he chairs the Landscape Design Department at the Ecole Nationale Supérieure du Paysage in Versailles. He is a frequent lecturer across Europe, has been a visiting critic at the Royal Academy of Fine Arts in Copenhagen, the Academy Van Bouwkunst in Amsterdam, the Harvard Graduate School of Design, the Technische Universität in Berlin, and the Moscow Institute of Architecture. Recent projects of his professional practice include the Invaliden Park in Berlin, the Parc des Six Arpents in Pierrelaye, and the Ilôt de Jeanne D'Arc garden in Paris.

Douglas Hollis is an artist who works with natural phenomena, including wind, water, and sound in an "ongoing attempt to create oasislike places where people may pause and catch their spiritual breath." He has worked on many publicly sponsored projects throughout the United States and abroad, and collaborated with prominent artists, architects, and landscape architects. Hollis has taught special studios at the Harvard Graduate School of Design, the University of Virginia, and the University of California, San Diego. He speaks frequently at public forums on the subject of public art and interdisciplinary collaboration, and has served on the board of the San Francisco Exploratorium and the Headlands Center for the Arts. His works include "A Sound Garden" in Seattle, "Rain Column" in San Francisco, and "Listening Vessels" in Raleigh, North Carolina.

Ricardo Legorreta's distinguished architectural career spans four decades. He studied architecture at the National University of Mexico and worked for José Villagran, becoming Villagran's partner in 1955. In 1963 he formed his own office, Legorreta Arquitectos. He has completed architectural projects throughout the world, including numerous libraries and institutional buildings in the United States. He has participated as an invited competitor for landmark international projects, and he is a member of the Pritzker Prize Committee.

Michael Manwaring is one of the leading practitioners of environmental graphic design. Integrating traditional graphic design with objects that make up the built environment. Manwaring has helped to establish environmental graphics as an important new discipline. Early involvement in exhibitions and sign-system design led to opportunities such as an art commission by the city of San Francisco for an interpretive environmental graphics program, including poetry and cultural and natural history for the Embarcadero Promenade along the San Francisco waterfront. The work of his firm, the Office of Michael Manwaring, for civic and corporate facilities has set a new standard for graphics in the environment. His work was featured in the first exhibition of graphic design at the San Francisco Museum of Modern Art. He is an adjunct professor of design at the California College of Arts and Crafts, where he received the Distinguished Faculty Award.

Elizabeth K. Meyer is an associate professor at the University of Virginia, where she chairs the Graduate Department of Landscape Architecture and teaches studio courses as well as lectures in modern landscape architecture practice and theory. She has served on the faculty of Harvard University. Professional experience includes affiliations with Michael Vergason and Associates, Hanna/Olin, and EDAW. She is currently writing a book entitled *The Margins of Modernity*.

Mary Miss has been a leader in redefining public sculpture since the 1970s. Her architecturally based vision has been instrumental in shifting how public art is viewed from the monument to aspects of landscape and the importance of site. In 1987 she completed South Cove in Battery Park City in New York. She is currently working on the renovation of the 14th Street Union Square Subway Station in New York City and the La Brea Tar Pit site in Los Angeles. She recently completed Greenwood Pond Double Site, a demonstration wetland in Des Moines, Iowa, on the grounds of the Des Moines Art Center. Her works are in the permanent collections of the Fogg Art Museum at Harvard University, the San Diego Museum of Art, California, and the Museum of Modern Art and the Solomon R. Guggenheim Museum in New York City.

Laurie Olin has worked in architectural and landscape offices in Seattle, New York, and London. With his firm the Olin Partnership in Philadelphia, he has been engaged in landscape design and planning consultation to internationally renowned design firms such as Pei Cobb Freed & Partners, Eisenman Architects, Skidmore Owings, & Merrill, Frank O. Gehry, and Hardy Holzman Pfeiffer. He has served on the faculty of landscape architecture and regional planning at the University of Pennsylvania, and as chair of the Department of Landscape Architecture at the Graduate School of Design at Harvard University. He is currently adjunct professor at the Graduate School of Fine Arts at the University of Pennsylvania. He is a John Simon Guggenheim Fellow and Fellow of the American Academy in Rome.

Adèle Naudé Santos is an architect and urban designer who believes architecture must transcend functional accommodation, and that it must be socially as well as contextually responsible. Her beliefs are expressed in all of her projects and particularly in her design of low-cost housing. She was the founding dean of the New School of Architecture

at the University of California, San Diego, and is currently a professor at the University of California, Berkeley. She has also held professorships within the graduate programs of Harvard University, Rice University, and the University of Pennsylvania, where she chaired the Department of Architecture from 1981 to 1987. Her work includes the Yerba Buena Gardens Children's Center in San Francisco and housing projects in Los Angeles and in Kitakyushu, Japan.

Martha Schwartz combines her fine arts and landscape architecture background in pursuit of opportunities to elevate landscape design to the level of fine art. The work of her Cambridge, Massachusetts-based firm has been repeatedly recognized through design award programs and in widespread publications and gallery exhibitions. She is an adjunct professor of landscape architecture at the Harvard University Graduate School of Design, has served as a visiting resident at Radcliffe College and the American Academy in Rome, and is a frequent and popular lecturer, both nationally and internationally.

Marc Treib, a professor of architecture at the University of California, Berkeley, for almost two decades, lectures and writes about architecture, landscape, and graphic design. His publications include *A Guide to the Gardens of Kyoto; Modern Landscape Architecture, A Critical Review; Sanctuaries of Spanish New Mexico; The Houses of William Wurster; The Regional Gardens of the United States; and Garrett Eckbo: Modern Landscapes for Living.*

Invaliden Park. Berlin, Germany

Parc des six Arpents. Paris, France

Christophe Girot Paysagiste   Parc des Six Arpents. Paris, France

Jardin de L'Ilôt Jeanne d'Arc. Paris, France

11

Douglas Hollis and Charles Fahlen

A Tidal Park. Port Townsend, Washington

12

Legorreta Arquitectos

Private Residence. Sonoma, California

Office of Michael Manwaring

Embarcadero Promenade. San Francisco, California

14

Mary Miss

Greenwood Pond: Double site. Des Moines, Iowa

Robert F. Wagner Jr. Park. New York City, New York

Olin Partnership

Vila Olimpica. Barcelona, Spain

16

Adèle Naudé Santos and Associates with Jacob/Wyper Architects

Albright College Center for the Arts. Reading, Pennsylvania

Sound Wall. Miami, Florida

17

Martha Schwartz, Inc.

The Littman Wedding. Deal, New Jersey

As designers, we were raised in a culture of criticism. Such criticism is inextricable from a studio-based curriculum carried out through individual critiques, group pin-ups, and public reviews. While lectures and demonstrations offer certain lessons, such as the teaching of history and technology or specific drawing and modeling techniques, the majority of one's education as a designer of landscapes occurs by learning through doing, and then listening to a critique of one's work. Whether artist, architect, or landscape architect, criticism is a normal part of our indoctrination into our disciplines. Through criticism, the instructor introduces the student to a descriptive world, frames the boundaries of their shared discipline, demystifies the act of design, and sets evaluative standards.

The critic can assist the reader, or visitor, by reframing "designed landscape objects" as "designed landscape works." The designed landscape object is whole, completed by its creator, and described by her or him as a piece, a totality. The critic expands the world of the designed landscape object through interpretation, through explication of the content and context of the work. She finds meaning not only in the complete forms and spaces of the designer's markings on the paper and the land, but in the relationship between those marks and the context. That context is defined by the critic in three ways: the designer's body of works; the traditions of the field (landscape architecture, architecture, sculpture, theater); and the tensions of the time—the immediate cultural milieu.

Through this contextualization, the landscape is transformed from an autonomous designed object into textural work that is interwoven and intermingled with the world. The object becomes a fragment, a thread, a strain that is illuminated by its relationship to the surroundings. Landscape as object becomes landscape in situ, a place. In Arthur Danto's terms, the critic "identifies the thoughts that give life" to the work.

As a critic of designed landscapes, not paintings, interior architecture, or literature, I am curious about the place of a project, not its canvas or base or page. Where is this landscape? What is adjacent to it? What previously existed on the site? How much of that found landscape was demolished and/or appropriated by the designer? What did the designer do in response to this place that wasn't present in her or his previous projects? As a critic of the designed landscape, I am curious about the time of the project. How will the project change over time? How does it register that change from day to day, season to season, year to year? How does the project reflect and refract the broader tensions of its time—changing ideas about nature, the city and suburb, public and private, subjectivity (the degree to which a user or inhabitant is not universal, but specific and constructed through gender, minorities, ethnicity)? How does the designer's position about his or her time inform the ways he or she explores and represents the project in drawings, diagrams, collages, and models?

Since I perceive the designed landscape in textural relationship to its time and place, since I differentiate it from other disciplines through this lens, the act of criticism requires more than familiarity with the published documents generally made available about a project. Few journals today are committed to documentation of more than designed landscape objects. In fact, most can barely manage to document a landscape scene or vignette. Plans, sections, axonometrics, and sequential perspectives keyed into photographs are rare in landscape publications. Detailed sections and axonometrics depicting construction techniques, standard in architectural journals, are relegated to issue-specific columns ("technology") and not considered a design concern. Panoramic photographs that more closely approximate the human cone of vision than do 35 millimeter photographs are rare. And photographs of the preconstruction site, or its nearby context are banished to dead files in a firm's basement.

Reflections on the First Designed Landscape Forum
Elizabeth K. Meyer

"A work of art is composed of a material object given life by a structure of thought, much as a human person may be regarded as a body animated by a soul. Criticism, in its highest vocation, identifies the thoughts that give life to a work or set of works."
Arthur Danto, *The State of the Art*

So how is a critic to work? By ferreting out these documents, by visiting the site. And what if such deliberation is not possible, as in the review of the work presented in this volume? With great humility, tentativeness, and equivocation.

During the Designed Landscape Forum that met in San Francisco in November 1996, I participated in one of four groups that reviewed and critiqued the projects discussed publicly in the San Francisco Museum of Modern Art. On Friday, the day of reviewing and selecting projects, our group was comprised of Michael Manwaring, an environmental graphic designer from San Francisco, architect and landscape architect Christophe Girot from Paris, and me, a landscape architect from Charlottesville, Virginia. All three of us are designers and educators. We were joined on Saturday for the symposium by Mexican architect Ricardo Legorreta.

While I do not pretend that my position as a critic speaks for the group, I can attest to the apprehension we all felt in reviewing more than two hundred projects so quickly and superficially. The quickness can be easily corrected in the next Forum's schedule, but the superficiality cannot, without some cooperation from the designers who submit their projects.

Few of the project descriptions included statements of design intent. Most were blandly written, perhaps for an office brochure or marketing endeavor. Ideas about the landscape, about our generation's contested definitions of nature and culture, ecology and art were not to be found. Instead, we were left with impoverished verbal descriptions of formal and informal, hardscape and softscape. Eventually, we found ourselves ignoring the texts and trying to find content and invention in the slides projected in front of us.

I relay this invisible part of the process to underscore how we arrived at a few projects to present to the symposium the following day. We did not discuss the primary concerns and trends of today, and look for work that illustrated those concerns. Rather, we identified works that moved us, and then tried to find a way to describe them to others. This led us to categories that are not comprehensive in their definition of the state of our art. But our process did lead us to select both works we knew and those we didn't know previously, enriching our sense of the fields and figures who are creating the designed landscape today.

Milestones and benchmarks

Among the eighty-some projects we reviewed, we identified three that stood out as exemplars of design intention realized in landscape form and space. The first, South Cove, designed by Susan Child in association with Mary Miss and Stan Eckstut, is well-known to most in the Designed Landscape Forum audience. A fragment of the Battery Park City Hudson River esplanade, South Cove defines the water's edge as amorphous, changing, and spatial with its multiple layers of piers, rails, and walks. Wooden boardwalks replace the asphalt-block-paved walks of the first phase of Battery Park City's esplanade. Displaced shoreline boulders and billowing Rosa rugosa hedges line the upland side of the boardwalk, evoking a preurban history of the site. At the southern end of the cove, a metal stair enveloped by an open framework crown provides access to a balcony overlooking the boardwalk and the harbor beyond. The boardwalk's surface peels back as it spirals out into the water, revealing structural beams under the esplanade that cantilevers over the river while simulating land. What appeared to be solid ground is actually thin surface.

This project is not only an addition to the master-planned urban precinct; it is a built critique of Battery Park City's earlier mode of contextualism. It marks a moment in the 1980s when the idea of landscape as context was expanded to include more than the visual present, or some form of generic historicism. Instead, the notion of landscape as memory device, a repository of partial and fragmented memories, was constituted, explored, and built. A design strategy was employed that first revealed those memories, partially forgotten and imperfectly remembered, and then kept the narrative open-ended enough to allow for multiple decodings and interpretations. It encouraged active engagement of those who stroll along its promenade. Collaboration extended to the public.

At the same time, a very different type of design collaboration was taking place in Texas, where a master plan was created for a large corporate office park that would include retail and recreational areas. The team included landscape architect Peter Walker and his associates, and two architectural firms, Legorreta Arquitectos and Mitchell/Giurgola. This complex represents the first mature work of Walker's firm in its search for a "minimalist garden without walls." From the master plan to each building and site plan to the detail design of the courtyards and fountains to the layout of parking courts, the formal strategies of seriality and flatness work at every scale of design. The degree to which these strategies seamlessly accommodate the banal functions and needs of an office environment while creating spaces and surfaces of great beauty astounds those of us who appreciate the difficulty of carrying out design intention at so many levels.

The last of this triad, Schwartz, Smith, Meyer's Yorkville Park, had recently been featured on the cover of *Landscape Architecture* magazine, so while new, it was also well-known. Remarkable on many levels, we were impressed with the team's decision to create a landscape-scaled curio case, a cabinet of Canadian landscape experiences with a geometric and spatial meter derived from the adjacent row houses and city blocks. Instead of trivializing nature through miniaturization, or simulating nature's appearance but not its scale or systems, the designers identified the salient materials, spaces, and most important, the phenomena associated with the various types of Canadian landscape, and captured those in urban boxes as a stamp collector would fill a scrapbook, or a botanist an herbarium. Here an urban construct of nature was defined and made manifest through the designed landscape. Formal space with its clear, restrained, geometric rhythms and phenomenal place—full of tactile, material, and ephemeral characteristics—coexist, enriching one another and the neighborhood.

These three projects reminded us of the substance and accomplishments of the 1980s, establishing benchmarks and milestones as we reviewed the other work.

Landscape as irony

When thinking of the landscape, one conjures up images of spaces vaster than those designed in architecture and art. Yet three projects that caught our attention condensed their power into minute dimensions, the thinness of the surface of the ground. Jeanine Centuori and Karen Bermann's African American Burial Ground was the winner of a recent competition to memorialize a cemetery discovered during the construction of a federal building project. Centuori and Bermann's proposal, presented with computer-altered photographs, would transform the sidewalks around this building into commemorative surfaces. These common surfaces, which connect the world of the living and the underworld, were appropriated for commemoration. Manhole covers carry text about the site's history, and in doing so become memory devices. The space between buildings and the curb is transformed into a mosaic of encrusted shards and fragments of everyday life—dishes, bowls, pots—brought to the site by members of the New York community.

This practice of covering a grave with household effects, common in African graves, was transported across the Atlantic Ocean by those enslaved in the seventeenth and eighteenth centuries. These sacred sites, marked by everyday things, were a place of passage and communication, a border between life and death. Centuori and Bermann resurrect this practice, adapting it to a collective scale in an urban context. Irony inscribed on the surface of the city's walks connects and separates that past and this present, the visible and the invisible, the known and the nameless, the majority and the marginal.

Rob Weller and his associates combined wit and irony in their forecourt for the German Institute of Standards (DIN). Thanks to Girot's involvement in our jury, we decoded the enigmatic dark horizontal stone tablet, the size of a plaza, that displayed scrambled text beneath a thin surface of flowing water. Scaled to the proportions of a sheet of standard legal paper, even the landscape's surface adhered to the controlling standards of DIN, which regulates many manufactured items. As DIN's employees toil in their offices to regulate and control even more items and processes of production, they can gaze at the landscape surface outside their offices, which initially seems to comply with their desire for order and precision. From this spot of privilege above, one can see just below the thin surface of running water a stone rectangle full of letters which comprise not words, but nonsense and disorder. All the regulations in the world cannot order the thoughts written on this standard page. The landscape surface denotes nothing without humankind's projection of values and ideas onto it in the form of built or designed interventions. This object is transformed into a work through its acknowledgment and ironic commentary on its surroundings.

Mother Ditch was a performance piece that took place within the culverted Los Angeles River one autumn day and night in 1995. Located at the intersection of two regulated flows, that of the river and that of immigrants, the performance created a "narrative mosaic" of this marginalized natural and cultural space. The evening performance was marked by light and text that transfigured the river ditch into a place of spectacle. The power of the work resides in its intensification of the qualities of a place through the choreography of light, music, and movement as well as in the projection of text onto a surface that is usually invisible, albeit indispensable, to life in the city. The ephemeral nature of the work, short-lived and not repeated, is partially responsible for the poignancy this project evokes. A fleeting event lingers in one's memory, leaving a residue in the landscape, invisible but real. Like the African American Burial Ground, Mother Ditch renders an ordinary space extraordinary.

All these projects require the participation of others to decode them, to unfold them. They defy objectification. They revel in the performative possibilities of public places.

Constructed sites

The designed landscape is frequently a collaborative effort, and at its best, the result is a place that defies categorization by disciplines or professions. It simply becomes a memorable place, not a building or a site. Such is the case with two museums and a research institute. While conditioned by individual programs and locales, each of these projects includes a phase of conceptual design that design theorists such as Kenneth Frampton and Carol Burns have called "the constructed site." Between the act of locating the parcel and designing the volume and massing of the building, each carefully shapes the ground plane, thus challenging the boundaries between inside and outside, building and landscape. The result is a highly sculptural figuring of both the ground itself and the spaces between ground, wall, and sky.

In BOORA Architects' Cheney Cowles Museum in Spokane, Washington, this strategy produces a complex that defies the idea of a building as an object in space. Described and conceived with geological metaphors, the museum seems to grow out of the ground itself, an earthwork made habitable. In Mario Schjetnan's Museo de

las Culturas del Norte in Chuhuahua, the habitable earthwork was the response to an extraordinary Pueblo archeological site. Requiring the museum for interpretive exhibits, but fearful of the impact of the construction on the desert valley, the structure was set five feet below the ground. The entrance ramps down into the earth. Within the museum, courtyard spaces bring light and air into the complex. Perhaps the most enchanting room is an atrium gallery that displays the surrounding soil strata in glass cases that also act as skylights, bringing in sunlight from above. The mixing of light and dark, air and earth through this crystalline prism conjures up memories of the world outside, above and below, as well as the world before, buried and excavated. It is a space Robert Smithson would have appreciated; the earth is transformed through its encasement and illumination into the medium of preservation, revelation, and memories.

The Neurosciences Institute in La Jolla has been extensively published as Todd Williams and Billie Tsien have increasingly been recognized as two of the most talented architects of their generation. One can trace the influences on their work to the roof gardens of Le Corbusier and the courtyards of Noguchi. But those influences alone do not ensure a built landscape of beauty, well-integrated with interior architecture. One only needs to visit Williams and Tsien's latest complex building and site ensemble, Hereford College at the University of Virginia, to appreciate the contributions of landscape architect collaborator William Burton (and the client) on the La Jolla project. Where the spaces between the UVA residential halls are awkward in both scale and proportion, and the earthwork and grading crude, those at the Neurosciences Institute are sublime in their simultaneous abstraction and craftsmanship.

These three projects constructed a site instead of locating a building as object. They made memorable places rather than a building or landscape exclusively. Their work is site specific.

The craft of landscape architecture

Two more projects—Robert Murase's Collins Circle in Portland, Oregon and Janice Hall's Murmuring Flow, in southwestern Connecticut—one civic and one residential—are substantial and enduring. As carefully built as they were conceived, they impressed us for their tectonics as well as their imagination. Murase took on Collins Circle, a residual traffic circle, as a sculptural problem. Assembling the circle out of cut stone, he formed the invisible space into a mass so tactile and heavy that it cannot help but be a major orientation device within the neighborhood. The sumac grove with its coarse branching structure, ability to withstand harsh conditions, and spreading root system is a fitting complement to the dry heavy stone surface comprising individual stones closely fit, but not mortared together.

The second project is even more surreal than the first. As we looked at the slides, we were convinced that the tray was jumbled. What was that dry stone stream doing in that Georgian house's garden? Where did it come from? Where was it going? For 300 feet it intermingled, tangled, tumbled, and flowed across the garden and along a wall, encountering a terrace and provoking those peeking out of the house's windows. An unlikely success, a concept that sounds too diagrammatic, too naive, too cartoonlike, this project is carried by the designer's attention to scale, detail, and siting. It is both a powerful earthwork and a garden folly.

These two projects were anomalies in a day full of slide trays with images of landscapes built quickly for clients with short-term return on their minds. Ever cognizant of this postmodern culture we inhabit, a culture of the spectacle and the facade, we were pleased to find a few projects built to last, and worthy of lasting. They gave the ground a presence, a figure with physical beauty that evoked associations with the region, and in doing so made ordinary sites memorable.

Didactic landscapes

Since the Designed Landscape Forum poster invited a range of people to submit work, from graphic designers and photographers to architects and garden designers, we felt compelled to look closely at landscapes that were not traditional built places, but were paper works, temporary works, referential works, and empowering works. Why? In order for public and professional perceptions of the landscape to become more accepting of strategies that aim to do more than beautify, a different type of designed landscape work is needed. Exhibitions, publications, reconstructions, reinterpretations, negotiations, and collaborations are called for.

Four projects exemplify diverse techniques for making the designed landscape more visible to the public. Duke Reiter's temporary exhibit about the Boston Harbor Islands creates a spatial interpretation of this archipelago's urban plight. Highly visible but unreachable, the islands evoke romantic flights of fancy in Boston's collective consciousness. In contrast, Reiter's exhibit underscores the vital connections between the Harbor Islands and the metropolis, cultural and geological. As the islands become museum pieces like those crafted by Reiter for his show (due to recent National Park Service acquisition and interpretation of the islands), what role will they play in the cultural imagination of Boston's citizens when they are managed and curated? This installation is an excellent example of how art works can serve as provocative tools for public education, and probe with a degree of intensity and subtlety not possible in written commentary or criticism.

Dean Cardasis' Plastic Garden represents an equally enigmatic landscape, albeit one less well-known outside the discipline of landscape architecture. The project, for all its response to a 1990s client and site, appears to be a reconstruction of a modular garden type designed by James Rose, the maverick Modernist.

Sarah Vance's graphic design for the first few publications for Spacemaker Press has brought to the publication of landscape works a degree of visual literacy that is usually reserved for architecture and art. The large-format color photographs immerse a reader in a moment of the place, while the drawings and small vignettes provide conceptual understanding of the whole. The ability to both imagine the character of the place and the spatial structure of the site plan is key to knowing a landscape work. I look forward to additional publications designed by Vance, and hope that she can create a format that includes drawings and contextual maps as thoughtfully.

Finally, Walter Hood's careful documentation of the process behind his work at Lafayette Square expands our sense of a didactic landscape to include the design phase of a project. While working within a University of California, Berkeley, tradition of community participation, he is not equating that participation with a design. Rather, by educating himself and the community about the collective memory of a place, he is building a consensus about the significance of the project. With this shared understanding in place, Hood is shaping a space for a designer of public spaces to actually represent the highest of civic intentions instead of merely accommodate the lowest common denominator. Public sector work hasn't looked so promising in decades.

These projects allowed Girot, Legorreta, Manwaring, and me to take a snapshot of the designed landscape in the last decade of the twentieth century. Interests and concerns that have percolated in the design and art worlds for the last quarter century—a concern for natural process and ecological literacy; a recognition of the landscape's cultural and historical content as well as ecological structure; a desire to consider the landscape as a text that can be marked, re-marked, and written upon; a rediscovery of the landscape's shared (and transgressible) boundaries with architecture and art; a commitment to the craft as well as conception of landscape—are manifest in a number of significant designed landscapes.

Looking ahead to the next Designed Landscape Forum

This legacy is rewarding, and yet I left the event in November wanting. As these once provocative and new ways of reading the landscape have infiltrated and redirected design practice, I yearn for more practitioners to seek the challenges presented by our time. Our bookstores, libraries, and theaters offer us a lens into the contested terrain of the late-twentieth-century landscape that we inhabit and shape through our daily rituals and routines. Urbanists now admit that agricultural conservation is key to the vitality of the city. Sprawl is destructive to both city and farm. Cultural critics comment on the homogeneity of our urban peripheries and offer nostalgic visions of pre-interstate communities as an antidote. Others revel in the placelessness of suburbia and embrace the globalization of local economies and cultures. Scholars and activists in philosophy, literature, art history, and cultural geography are mesmerized by the role of landscape/nature/wildnerness in our culture. *The New York Times* announces that ecocriticism has replaced cultural studies and deconstruction in the halls of academe.

As the meaning, value, and constructs of nature evolve in response to the contingencies of everyday life—the communication technologies that connect near and far, the recognition of the power of humankind to disturb our habitat, and the disbelief that we can escape civilization regardless how high, deep, or distant we are from human settlement—shouldn't landscape architects and other designers of the landscape be trying to interpret those debates in the very forms, surfaces, and spaces of our work?

Much of the designed landscape conceived today suffers from our lack of engagement in the intellectual, cultural, and scientific debates outlined above. We, the designers of the built landscape, are not constrained by lack of intention, talent, skill, or opportunity. We are constrained by conceiving of our work through hackneyed phrases (formal and informal, hardscape and softscape, man-made and natural) instead of through engagement with the tensions of our time. We are also constrained by conceiving and representing our work with graphic techniques best relegated to public presentations (and ironically dependent on a medium that destroys the very environment we purport to protect). There is no reason to design and draw with the same tool needed to make a site plan legible at a public meeting. Why aren't we seeing more models and perspectives employed as design tools versus presentation tools?

Thirty years ago Lawrence Halprin said we design static spaces because that is what we know how to draw. He's still right. We need to take up his challenge to develop ways of representing experience as well as structure, flux, and time as well as space. In our roles as critics, we hope not simply to make our readers aware of this plight. We hope to be part of the realignment of our practice.

The designed landscape is a genre that is especially well-suited to the challenges of representing our culture's complex relationship with our planet; situating our bodies in the present, the tangible, sensuous now; and imagining social spaces for exposure to others. It is a genre that continues to motivate us, move us, and compel us to not only design, teach and write about, but live in, this world. The intensity of this lived experience is dependent on our exposure to more works like these mentioned here. We welcome those encounters, and the reveries they evoke. They bind us to the world, and its structures of thought, at the same time they illuminate the boundaries and reaches of our own disciplines.

Richmond Residence
Richmond, Massachusetts
Child Associates

Family Burial Ground
Troy, Ohio
Child Associates

The Esplanade Condos
Cambridge, Massachusetts
Child Associates

Arch of the Oaks
Portland, Oregon. Lee Kelly with
Mitchell Nelson Welborn Reimann

Pukinmäki McDonald's Restaurant
Helsinki, Finland
Jerry Coburn, Penna Saarikoski

Garden with a Blue Gate
Saratoga, California
Chris Jacobson

Residence
Boxford, Massachusetts
Charlotte Present

Equinox
McHenry County, Illinois
George Voegel

In Search of Understanding
Palatine, Illinois
George Voegel

Garden of the Four Elements
San Francisco, California
Chip Sullivan

Civic Center Viewing Chamber
San Francisco, California
Chip Sullivan

Safari Park Hotel
Nairobe, Kenya
Belt Collins

Durfee Gardens
Amherst, Massachusetts
Dean Cardasis and Associates

Carriage House Garden
Amherst, Massachusetts
Joseph Volpe Associates

Brooke's Garden
Jason Christopher

The Rique Project
Angra dos Reis, Rio de Janeiro, Brasil
Frederick L. Gregory, Roberto Gonçalvez

Disease, Fire, Deer, and Drought
California Garden Fights Back
Chris Jacobson

Painted Steel Chair
San Francisco, California
Nancy Owens

Las Huertes
San Francisco, California
Nancy Owens

Stonegate Recreation Center Entrance
Scottsdale, Arizona
Paradigm Affiliates

23

Frog and the Ball
Charleston, South Carolina
Design Works

Port Orleans & Dixie Landings Retreat
Walt Disney World, Florida
RTKL

Reston Town Center
Reston, Virginia
RTKL

Twin Peaks Project
San Francisco, California
John Denning, Brigitte Micmacker

LEF Foundation
Napa Valley, California
Lutsko Associates

Delandscape
Ruey Y. Chen

IBM Almaden Research Laboratory
San Jose, California
The SWA Group

Silicon Graphics Shoreline Entry Site
Mountain View, California
The SWA Group

Bacon Mattes Residence
Traverse City, Michigan
Jeffrey Inaba, Apisek Wongvasu,
Tim Archambault

Papyrus Library
Ron Wigginton Land Studio

Union Bank Building Star Troughs
La Jolla, California
Ron Wigginton Land Studio

Rutherford Square
Rutherford, California
Ron Wigginton Land Studio

Fenceline Artifact
Denver International Airport
Sherry Wiggins, Buster Simpson,
Jim Logan

Pool as Art
Mill Valley, California
Raikes Landscape Company

S. L. Horsford & Company
Shopping Complex
St. Kitts, West Indies
Eustace Hobson Associates

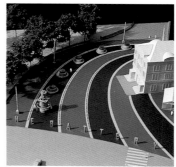

Temporary Plaza, Pier A
New York City, New York
Ken Smith

24

Residential Community
Potrero Heights, California
Jeffrey Miller

Moonen-Addis Design
Berkeley, California
Jeffrey Miller

Wisconsin Workers Memorial
Milwaukee, Wisconsin
Terese Agnew, Mary Zebell

Professor Longhair Square
New Orleans, Louisiana
David Tureau

Hyatt Regency at Gainey Ranch
Scottsdale, Arizona
The SWA Group

Intel Corporation
Santa Clara, California
The SWA Group

Ronald Reagan Presidential Library
Ventura County, California
The SWA Group

The Arbors at Maitland Summit
Orlando, Florida
Dix Nance, Inc.

Ross's Landing
Chattanooga, Tennessee
EDAW

Canal City Hakata
Fukuoka, Japan
EDAW

The Terraces Continuing Care Facility
Los Gatos, California
EDAW

The Johnston Residence—
Lemon Scented Days in the Sun
April Philips

AIDS Memorial
Key West, Florida
Karen Bermann, Jeanine Centuori, with
Russell Rock and Phil Appleton

Cloud Gardens Park
Toronto, Canada
Baird Sampson

Soundscape Lawn and
Garden Demonstration
Seattle, Washington
Kathleen Wadden, Ecos Atelier

Sound Playground
South Bronx, New York
Bill and Mary Buchen

25

Green Acres
Trenton, New Jersey
Athena Tacha

Douglass Spark Park
Houston, Texas
Office of Alan Berger

Ilus W. Davis Civic Park
Sasaki Associates

Babelsberg Media City
Babelsberg, Germany
Sasaki Associates

Merging
Case Western University
Cleveland, Ohio
Athena Tacha

Bet Gabriel Garden
Sea of Galilee, Israel
Ulrik Plesner, Dan Wajnman

African Garden
Brooklyn, New York
Alice Adams

The Roundabout
Philadelphia, Pennsylvania
Alice Adams

East River Esplanade
New York City
Thomas Balsley Associates

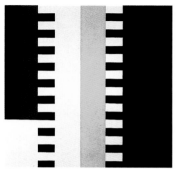

Khartoum
Mary Henry

Field of Corn
Dublin, Ohio
Malcolm Cochran

Untitled
Hussein Gamaan

Baltimore Washington Airport
Landscape Enhancement
Anne Arundel County, Maryland
Graham Landscape Architecture

"The Shade," Rodin Sculpture Relocation
Atlanta, Georgia
Lorenc Design

Sun, Wind, and Water Sculpture
Meridian Business Campus
Fort Lauderdale, Florida
Lorenc Design

Flight Sculptures
Birmingham, Alabama Airport
Lorenc Design

26

Tennessee Bicentennial Capitol Mall
Nashville, Tennesee
Tuck Hinton Architects

Ma and Pa Heritage Corridor
Hartford County, Maryland
Katherine Aldrich Adams

Bridges
Redwood Valley, California
Skip Gibbs, Katie Gibbs-Gengoux

Taylor Park Historic Riverwalk
Newport, Kentucky
Meyers Schmalenberger Meisner

NTT Motomachi Cred Plaza
Hiroshima, Japan
Yoji Sasaki, Ohtori Consultants

Suita Station Plaza
Suita City, Japan
Yoji Sasaki, Ohtori Consultants

One Sun Garden
Colorado State University
Fort Collins, Colorado
Abbey Wilson, Andrea Cummins

The Wishing Trees
Portland, Oregon
Fernanda D'Agostino

Visible Landscapes
Dixi Carrillo

Imagine The Option
Colorado State University
Fort Collins, Colorado
Shannon Bretthorst, Marcel Wilson

Recombinant Imagery
Robert Silance
RSCT Architecture and Design

Dreamy Draw Pedestrian Bridge
Phoenix, Arizona
Vicki Scuri Siteworks

Untitled
San Francisco, California
Delaney & Cochran

Telltale
Adelaide, Australia
Mark Robbins

Fort Mason Garden Show
San Francisco, California
Jill Gropp, Akiko Iishi

Beginnings
Ruth Rodman

Copenhagen Summer Landscape
Sung-Ja Cho

Landscape Sculptural Garden #1
Sung-Ja Cho

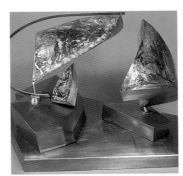

Sculptural Dialogue #2
Sung-Ja Cho

Children's Architectonic Playground
Sung-Ja Cho

Garden of Mysterious Matter
Duxbury, Massachusetts
Rebecca Krinke

Inside Out
Landscape Garden Show
San Francisco, California
Mary Tienken, Elizabeth Gourley

Visible Cities
Wellington Reiter

Poetic Light
Grand Central Terminal
New York City, New York
Louise Braverman

27

Three Omaha Stockyard Installations
Omaha, Nebraska
Cynthia Harper

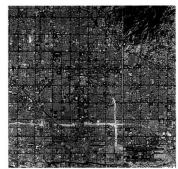

A Poetic of the Middle Landscape:
Phoenix, Arizona
Craig P. Verzone

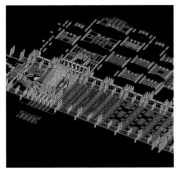

Rancho Mirage Civic Center
Arthur Golding and Associates

America the Beautiful
United States Pavillion World Expo
Seville, Spain
Antoine Predock

Curandera's Garden: Sur Y Norte
Edith Katz, Ada Medina

The Garden is Taking Wing
Caroline Lavoie, Daniel Gauthier

Maryland WWII Memorial
David Meyer, Karolos Hanikian

Landscape Photographs
Tom Lamb

28

Tualatin Hills Park
Beaverton, Oregon
BOORA Architects

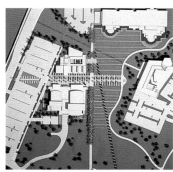

Fremont Cultural Arts Center
Fremont, California
BOORA Architects

The Soil That NY Rejected:
The Other United Nations
Anu Mathur, Dilip Da Cunha

Embarcadero Open Space,
Waterfront, and Transportation Project
San Francisco, California
Francesca S. Levaggi

Hilltop Residence
Office of H. Keith Wagner

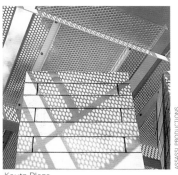

Kautz Plaza
University of Iowa
Iowa City, Iowa
Herbert Lewis Kruse & Blunck Architects

Sacramento Railyards Specific Plan
Sacramento, California
Roma Design Group

Pier 7
San Francisco, California
Roma Design Group

Suisan City Development Plan
Suisan City, California
Roma Design Group

Santa Monica Third Street Promenade
Santa Monica, California
Roma Design Group

The Four Relationships to Ground
Concord, Massachusetts
Christopher James Fannin

Ime Urban Natural Park
Boondang and Sungman, Korea
Hong-Kyu Kim, Shin-Hyun Choi

Port of Barcelona
Barcelona, Spain
Shawn Rickenbacker

Private Garden
San Francisco, California
Steven Abrahams

Business Park
Leipzig, Germany
Bernd Krüger, Hubert Möhrle

Beth Israel Chapel and Cemetery
Houston, Texas
Gary Leonard Strang

29

Beacon Street Urban Forest
Brookline, Massachusetts
Kaki Martin

Gravity Garden
Culver City, California
Pam Davis

Lachish River Park
Ashdod, Israel
Tichnun Nof Ltd.

Sears Parking Lot
Boston, Massachusetts
Betsy Boykin

Boston Harbor Islands National Park
Boston, Massachusetts
Sara Fairchild, Paula Meijerink

Scripps College Art Science Walk
Claremont, California
Pamela Burton & Company

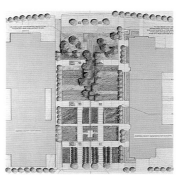

Los Angeles Civic Center
Los Angeles, California
Pamela Burton & Company

State Street Renovation
Chicago, Illinois
Skidmore, Owings & Merrill

LG Beijing
Beijing, People's Republic of China
Skidmore, Owings & Merrill

Benesse Island
Naoshima, Japan
Skidmore, Owings & Merrill

Glenview Naval Air Station Reuse Plan
Glenview, Illinois
Skidmore, Owings & Merrill

Center for Urban Horticulture
Seattle, Washington
Jones & Jones

Paris-Lexington Road
Paris to Lexington, Kentucky
Jones & Jones

Myombe Reserve, Busch Gardens
Tampa Bay Florida
Jones & Jones

Botanic Gardens
Singapore
Jones & Jones

Mountains to Sound Greenway
Puget Sound, Washington
Jones & Jones

30

The Consumers Lobby
Bothell, Washington
Richard Posner

Urban Acupuncture
Paris, France
Jim Williamson, Alexis Wreden,
Beth Whitaker

Photographs of the Designed Landscape
Susan Sutton Palmer

Wavewall in Green
Coney Island, New York
Edward L. Smyth

Landfall
Wilmington, Delaware
Edward L. Smyth

Community Center
Chenove, France
Vito Acconci & Studio

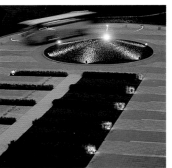

Fuji Canon Research Park
Mt. Fuji, Japan
Makoto Naborisaka, David Buck

Ayala Triangle
Manila, Philippines
Peter Walker William Johnson and Partners

Barnsdall Park Master Plan
Los Angeles, California
Peter Walker William Johnson and Partners

Longacres Park
Renton, Washington
Peter Walker William Johnson and Partners

Dwelling Wood
Christopher Reed

Five Clay Domes for Washington and Lee
Washington and Lee University
Lexington, Virginia
Stephen Korns

Lafayette Square Master Plan
Oakland, California
Walter Hood

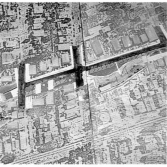
Courtland Creek Park
Oakland, California
Walter Hood

Rainbow Plaza in Edogawa Ward
Tokyo, Japan
Yoshiki Toda

Onomichi City Junior College
Hiroshima Prefecture, Japan
Yoshiki Toda

31

Beppu Municipal Office Square
Ohita Prefecture, Japan
Yoshiki Toda

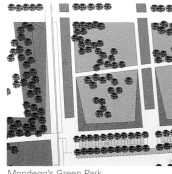
Mondego's Green Park
Coimbra, Portugal
PROAP Landscape Architecture

Santa Sofia Park
PROAP Landscape Architecture

Marina De Lagos
PROAP Landscape Architecture

WWII Memorial, Forest of Memory
Ryoko Ueyama

Live Not One Evil: Anti-Facist Theme Park
Richard Posner

Landsdowne
The GNU Group

Alan Sutera
Jakarta, Indonesia
The GNU Group

How might the various practices of landscape architecture advance and evolve during the next few decades? Is it imaginable that landscape might enjoy increased visibility and efficacy in cultural affairs, or is it perhaps easier to foresee the field further marginalized, confused, and even rendered obsolete by the forces that are sweeping global society?

In sight of the next millennium, and more than well aware of the uncertainty surrounding answers to the above questions, the Designed Landscape Forum has decided to seek out and promote works of landscape architecture that are "culturally ambitious." I believe this aim to be of the utmost importance for our field, but it is not without difficulty or ambiguity. In this essay, I want to expand on what is implied by this phrase, why it is so significant, and what future directions may prove fruitful in this regard.

The aspiration to achieve a culturally ambitious landscape is itself a lofty goal, especially for a field that is still struggling to gain collective identity among its members and general recognition by the public. Given the marginal role that landscape architecture plays in today's society, it might be naive or, at best, optimistic to believe that landscape architects could assume a prominent position in cultural and political affairs. After all, landscape has not played a particularly active role in culture for most of this century. Compared to the innovative explosion of modern communications and media technologies that pervade our time, landscape must appear to many as a rather antiquated medium, and its design a fringe activity sustained through the passions of a few quiet romantics and gentle nature lovers. Indeed, as an image that invokes a seemingly virtuous and innocent nature, landscape is typically viewed as the soothing antithesis, and therefore the compensating balance, to the placeless frenzy of technological life.

Consequently, the very idea that landscape might function as a forward-probing and critical instrument in the shaping of modern society must appear incongruous to many. In this pervasive but erroneous view, landscape is simply a venue for escapism and retreat, not a medium of cultural advance and innovation.

Moreover, it is hard to imagine a time in this century when landscape architecture was truly ambitious and revolutionary in its effects, at least compared with the remarkable transformations of early-twentieth-century art and architecture. Whereas Frederick Law Olmsted, Robert Moses, and Ian McHarg come to mind as visionary landscape architects and public officials who made enormous contributions to society, these individuals represent only a small, albeit significant, handful of people, and are not typical of today's more clerical, hyperprofessionalized landscape architects.

Themes of utopia, heroic art, and political prowess are more associated with architecture, urban planning, and civil engineering than with the softly mannered landscape architect, who is more likely to be associated with passive elements such as nature, plantings, and scenery than with cultural ambition. It is probably fair to say, in fact, that painters, filmmakers, earth artists, and even ecoactivist groups have propelled the very idea of landscape more deeply into the imagination of contemporary culture than have twentieth-century landscape architects, who have appeared to be more preoccupied with pragmatic techniques of scenic or environmental amelioration than with advancing a culturally critical and creative vision for the landscape project.

There are those, of course, who believe that landscape architecture should be more concerned with the stewardship of the natural world than with the cultivation of culture and that this ecological imperative characterizes the success and relevance of the profession during recent decades. Such proponents will likely protest that the promotion of culturally ambitious landscapes is largely irrelevant, more the domain of elitist art practices than inherent in the practical commitments of healing the earth.

This protest represents an unfortunate and confused schism. One might argue, as would McHarg, for instance, that to restore the biotic systems of the earth is culturally ambitious, and aspires to nothing less than the design of a systematic and reciprocal fit between human patterns of settlement and ecological life. At the levels of sociopolitical and professional relevance, such a vision is unequivocally clear-sighted for a world whose population continues to grow while its resources are diminishing. But while I believe that topics of environmental planning need to be more creatively explored by landscape architects, the difficulty remains that most environmental advocates typically put nature before culture, looking to a world outside, and not within. And, as Samuel Taylor Coleridge observed, to be "unchanged within and to see all changed without / Is a blank lot and hard to bear no doubt." Thus our societal and environmental problems (pollution, waste, overdevelopment) derive from our culturally constructed ways of knowing and seeing; to simply ameliorate the problem fails to adequately address its source: the cultural imagination, which so fundamentally conditions the ways in which we see and act in the world.

It is from this foundation that I remain committed to reinvigorating the landscape project as a means of critically intervening in cultural habit and convention. While I appreciate landscape as a historical product of culture, I am more interested in landscape architecture that actively produces culture. The emphasis shifts significantly from landscape as noun (as object or scene), to landscape as verb (as process or agent). This is why we must continue to speak of landscape as a temporal and interventionist art, as poetic production, as something within and not merely a prescription for external reality.

I am aware of some difficulty the reader may have in picturing what culturally ambitious landscape architecture might look like, or how, whatever form it takes, one might advance an alternative version of the landscape project in today's relatively indifferent social climate. But perhaps cultural ambition in landscape projects is less a matter of appearances and esthetic categories than an issue of strategy, a creative revision of the discipline's most basic tenets, scope, and modes of operation.

The idea of landscape, as with its various formations and practices, is subject to enormous shifts in meaning, content, and effect. As examples of Oriental, eighteenth-century European, or late-twentieth-century American versions of landscape show, the genre is not at all stable. Indeed, to assume that every society shares our American view of landscape, or even that other societies possess any version of landscape at all, is to wrongly impose on other cultures our own sensibility.

Consider Kenneth Clark's analysis of shifting landscape perceptions in his book *Landscape into Art*, in which he outlines a variety of landscape formations that range from the medievalist view of symbolism and Renaissance ideals of divine order, to Modernist themes of order and abstraction. Only in the epilogue does Clark infer the current situation through invoking new advances in science and imaging that cross scales and break with traditional categories. Clark outlines some of the innovative transformations of the landscape idea over time. He shows us that landscape, like painting or sculpture, is produced through the human imagination in speculative contact with the material world, and that this activity is open to new interpretation and practice. Here, landscape is not restricted to the physical world of topography, objects, and materials but is inextricably bound into a variety of representations across a range of media.

Thus, landscape space can never be separated from the landscape idea. Even untouched native areas of wilderness are landscapes to the degree that they are culturally understood and appreciated through their various representations (which may range from scientific accounts of flora and fauna to artists renderings in pigment or photograph). Thus, the environment—whether built or natural—is always apprehended (one might also say filtered or conditioned) through a variety of projections that collectively form the medium we call landscape.

In different ways, those preoccupied with the subject are finding that landscape is first and foremost an imaginative project, a speculative activity that conditions understanding and affects actions taken in the world. Whether in the form of maps, paintings, photographs, texts, movies, gardens, parks, earthworks, or urban infrastructures, the landscape project is historically layered as an immense treasure of often contesting fictions, ideas, and experiences. The degree to which this quarry of effects plays out in the larger cultural field is predicated upon the ability of landscape to align itself with and against the prevailing forces of the time. In this regard, the historical record shows that landscape has been a remarkably malleable phenomenon, appearing and signifying in markedly different ways across different times and cultures. And while those of us who are committed to landscape projects have a deep desire to see it more vigorously foregrounded in contemporary cultural affairs, there is no reason to assume that such a recovery would necessarily be to the benefit of society.

There are very valid reasons why, in fact, landscape ought to be courted with some skepticism. Consider, for instance, Raymond Williams' remark that "a working country is hardly ever a landscape," or Jean Francoise Lyotard's provocative claim that "to have a feeling for landscape you have to lose your feeling of place—a place is natural, but a landscape is an excess of presence." Both of these comments suggest that landscape has certain estranging characteristics (as in objectification and distancing) which, in turn, may be used to consolidate and represent certain dominant power interests (whether of aristocracy, political ideology, or market enterprise).

Some writers, John Barrell or W.J.T. Mitchell, for instance, describe a "dark side" of landscape, a moral and political darkness that derives from landscape's agency in erecting, veiling, and perpetuating various powers. Such veiling is rendered all the more effective because of the way in which landscape naturalizes its effects with time, concealing any signs of artifice or human will.

We live in a time when the landscape idea has lost a great deal of its imaginative and ethical force. It appears to me, judging by all of those buffer strips, planted screens, scenic renderings, and re-creations of nineteenth-century public space, that landscape has calcified into something passive, static, of-the-past, co-opted more for scenic compensation and commodification than for anything really penetrating. In its most commercial form, landscape architecture today plays a rather sad role in society, functioning more as a palliative and concealing screen for consumer pacification than as a critical art form actively engaged with the difficulties of contemporary life.

It is precisely an ambitious and visionary revival of the landscape project—the work of the speculative, the treatise, the manifesto, the delirious excitement and hybridization of ideas—that must be developed as an urgent alternative to the presently narrow-minded, hyperprofessionalized, impoverished landscapes of the clerical disciplines. There is a lot more one can elaborate upon here, but the point is simply to suggest that the full complexity of the landscape medium ought to be properly analyzed before any appraisal of contemporary landscape architectural practices can be made. Although landscape architects are primarily concerned with material and built interventions (as distinct from, say, paintings, natural history essays, or other verbal and visual representations), their work still occurs within a much larger landscape milieu that is cultural in origin and effect.

By this, I mean to invoke not only the contextual adjacencies and relationships between site and region, but also the broader arena of the landscape imagination. In building upon the many representations that comprise the landscape medium, I believe that the field may achieve increased efficacy in contemporary cultural affairs. And it is precisely the unnaturalness of the landscape medium, its constructed character in both ideas and physical terms, that ought to form the subject of contemporary landscape architectural research and practice.

Thus, for me at least, the Forum's criterion of "culturally ambitious" invokes a whole new kind of landscape architectural project, one that cannot just be limited to competently executed built work, but to work that innovates with regard to a larger critique and enrichment of the landscape medium itself.

Many on the Forum committee wished that more artists had submitted work for discussion, and indeed, many of the works that were submitted by artists provided the stimulus for a very thoughtful series of deliberations and ideas. But at the same time, the reliance upon artists to provide new and compelling ideas reveals a rather defeatist position with regard to landscape architectural innovation. Where are those specifically landscape architectural projects that deal creatively, at the level of art, with complex urban, programmatic, environmental, and cultural issues?

To be sure, the proficiency at craft and detail is clearly visible in the best of our profession's work, but craft without motivation seems merely technical to me. And it is here where the much-questioned role of theory and criticism in contemporary practice becomes of great importance, for it is only through the informed act of questioning through design (as distinct from prescriptive convention) that innovation at the cultural level is most likely to occur.

It was with many of these thoughts in mind that I, along with my colleagues on the panel, surveyed the more than two hundred submissions to the Designed Landscape Forum. What would be our criterion for judging work as culturally ambitious? What would be the marks of culturally ambitious work? And how might a prospectus or manifesto emerge with regard to charting future directions for the field? With the benefit of hindsight and reflection, I can characterize three essential measures—the *critical*, the *tactile*, and the *complex*—that, at least in part, guided our deliberations and point toward future directions for the field.

To what degree does a particular project assume an intelligent and inventive posture with regard to the circumstances of its production? And what previously unimagined possibilities are disclosed through landscape projection? Answers to these questions derive from operating at a level higher than simple problem-solving and formulaic site planning: at the level of ideas. This is the level of Emerson's "poetic excess," the territory beyond utility and economy, although not exclusive of them. Here, *criticism* is essentially a constructive and optimistic enterprise, not a negative, joyless task. There are many topics around which a critical practice may be focused: the various discourses of nature and ecology; issues of capitalism (especially landscape as scenic commodity); local and regional issues in a global world, and other such topical concerns.

Consequently, the need to gain increased knowledge of contemporary themes, as well as the ambition and confidence to somehow address them through landscape architecture, underscores the relevance of theory and criticism in design. Theory offers to designers a framework of critical questions and techniques around which their work might be motivated. Theory should not be associated solely with the linguistic medium, and neither should it be thought of as merely contemplative. The task of design inevitably implicates theory of one sort or another, and the kind of theory spoken of here is one that is both imaginative and productive. The critical practitioner begins with reflection, skepticism, unfulfillment, and then proceeds speculatively toward taking action.

The culturally ambitious landscape architect is therefore one who reflects, draws, and builds with critical prowess, one for whom theorizing, imaging, thinking, and building are one creative process. Today, more than ever, the field of landscape architecture embraces writers, critics, and artists, partly for their promotional and popularizing skills, and partly for their incisiveness with regard to situating the discipline culturally. But most of these activities occur after the design act, on reflection, whereas the kind of critical activity that I am advocating is one that precedes and accompanies the design process itself, one that is internal to the discipline. As with the field's of imaging and media techniques, the critical must evolve as a generative instrument, a medium.

In this regard, Michael Lehrer's design for the Barnsdall Hollywood Tower and the North Corner Park in Los Feliz presents a revision of monumentality and landmark signage in the otherwise undifferentiated flow of Hollywood Boulevard. Artist submissions by Andrea Wollensak (an essay on aerial surveillance and military landscapes) and B.J. Krivanek (Mother Ditch) provide other instances of critically motivated work. Still, these instances were few and far between, with most submissions failing to outline or acknowledge any critical frame of questioning or referencing in their work. If the landscape project is to resurface with any vigorous force, then it must be intelligently motivated by inquiring minds and agile conceptual formations.

Tactile materiality is intrinsic to landscape. Thus, the ideas and critical practices outlined above cannot simply operate at the verbal or narrational level; rather, they must communicate ontologically, through the spatial and tactile senses. Moreover, to place such emphasis upon kinesthetic and tactile experience (olfactory, haptic, and aural) provides a core of resistance to the commodifying impulse that reduces landscape to scenery or merely visual background. Deep and lasting in its effects, the tactile experience of landscape pervades the very soul of the material imagination. Whereas the scenic gaze tends to objectify and distance the subject, the tactile engages, sublimates, and draws one nearer to the experience of place. The tactile returns us literally to the intimacy of things, the warmth of wood and the coldness of metal, the musk of damp leaves and the balm of humid air, or the coarseness of volcanic rock and the polish of fossilized rock. And then there is the most palpable presence of the body's own momentum, gait, and weight as it passes from threshold to enclosure to horizon.

A plenitude of presence, the poetic plasticity of landscape form represents a means of assuring greater nearness between subject and object, almost to the point of complete dissolution, while avoiding the estranging distance of the scenic and consumptive effects of late capitalism. At the Forum, we saw a wonderful work by artist Mara Adamitz Scrupe, called Traversing Reverse Rivers. Here, on the banks of the Hudson River, the artist laid one thousand emergency water storage bags, filled with river water, and lit them from below by photocells that brightened and dimmed in relation to darkness. The slides submitted by the artist first showed the site, a woodland glade, prior to installation; the installation in daytime, a marvelously soft and watery carpet of rubbery pillows upon which to walk; the installation at dusk, with increasing illumination, eerie and mysterious; the strangely glowing, aqueous light at night; and then the flickering, diminished light at dawn. The final slide showed the site after the work had been removed, as if nothing had ever transpired.

Paolo Burgi's series of open spaces for a school in Ticino, Switzerland, captured the tactile effects of rainfall upon taut, stone surfaces. These hard, granite courtyards are extremely spare and minimal, and are conceived to transmit sheets of rainwater to strategically placed inlets and linear drains. As one moves through these extremely simple and refined spaces, a series of different ways in which the hydrological cycle moves with gravity is magically revealed.

In a more overtly representational way than Burgi's surfaces, Douglas Reed's Therapeutic Garden for Children also embodies a highly tactile mimesis of its larger situation. One can never appreciate this garden from a single vantage point, and neither does it make particularly beautiful photographs. Instead, the greater part of experiencing this design derives from moving through its softly contoured spaces, across its grass dew surfaces, slowly accumulating a range of incidents, discoveries, places of craft, and moments of pure pleasure. And, of course, the tactile is received in this garden through experience and motion; the landscape is not objectified but allowed to appear through the distractedness of its ambulant occupants. Consequently, as in the work of A.E. Bye, Janis Hall, or Michael Van Valkenburgh, the place eludes easy classification or representation; it always escapes.

By the *complex*, I mean to invoke a much more sophisticated range of issues and possibilities for the medium than most current design practices seem able or willing to embrace. To be effective in the twenty-first century, landscape architects will have to learn new and creative ways to work with the increasingly complicated forces that operate across a given terrain; the field will have to become more conversant with emerging ideas in science, art, philosophy, and urbanism—each of which are already outlining a whole new paradigm of complexity, network fields, global interrelationships, and morphogenesis. Indeed, once considered as separate and unrelated, the disciplines of biology, economics, and technology are becoming increasingly interrelational and analogous to one another, especially in terms of their temporal development and processes of formation. And, because of vast shifts in global patterns of capital accumulation, mobility of resources, and technology, and the rise of consumer economies, the contemporary metropolitan landscape tends to constitute itself as an evolving, nonorganic, and complex structure without hierarchical or linear organization. Space today is becoming less and less about Cartesian objecthood, and is emerging instead as fluid milieux, dynamic, polycentric, heterogeneous, indeterminate, and discontinuous. In this light, the various "stabilities" (spatial, temporal, legislative, social) of traditional design practices would appear to impede cultural evolution rather than to advance and enrich the complexities of difference, open-endedness, and indeterminacy.

Ironically, ecology serves as a great metaphor for understanding many of these cultural and economic processes of capitalism. The capacity of ecology to outline networks of interrelationship, to relate parts to one another and reveal a variety of interdependencies, to appreciate discontinuity as an ingredient of renewal, and to advance a vocabulary of time, network, flows, layers, and other such complex forces, makes it a particularly powerful framework for both analysis and projection. Landscape architects might assume a leading role in such developments if only they could move past ecology as solely a natural science (as if it were possible to separate nature from culture anyway). What is needed is an ecology of culture, an ecology wherein the creative ingenuity of the human imagination is allowed to innovate, to extend new hybrids, and to fully partake in the pure diversifying force of evolution.

One direct avenue of work here for landscape architects concerns infrastructure. Flexible and state-of-the-art infrastructure is increasingly the primary determinant of future development. The Sun Belt cities—Los Angeles, Phoenix, Houston, Atlanta, Miami—have emerged solely as the result of railroads and interstate highways, and their explicit infrastructural form allows them to respond with relative ease to changing needs and demands. These modern cities developed as a polycentric structure of dense cores, each oriented along the topological continuity of their various lifeline infrastructures. Capitalist production and investment centers more upon cities that are flexible, accessible, and, to some degree, novel, than around traditional, rigid structures that are simply too costly to retrofit. Consequently, cities and regions have had to invest in a range of new and open infrastructures in a bid to secure surplus capital and new alliances. Landscape architects ought to be at the forefront of these developments, leading the way, and not hired solely for scenic makeovers.

In the Forum, it was disappointing to see so little work that addressed these complex issues. It was even more disheartening to see some panelists promote art (defined solely in terms of formalist esthetics) above the more difficult, urbanistic issues of ecology, socioeconomics, programmatic innovation, or infrastructure. This may have occurred, at least in part, because of the totally uninspired and uncritical work that passed itself off as either ecological or infrastructural. Moreover, some artists did indeed address infrastructural issues, albeit contemplatively. Fernanda D'Agostino's Abundance and Scarcity project stakes out a cornfield and granary in an unusual ceremonial manner for a harvest dinner, pointing toward programs of cultivation and community events. Anna Valentina Murch's project (designed with Austin Tao and Bob Banaskeck) for the opening of a St. Louis Metro tunnel carpets the slopes and surfaces of the embankments with colored broken glass. The slopes are then lit in special ways with metal halide lighting, outlining a creative approach toward derelict or marginal sites, especially sites of passage, speed, and motion.

The one landscape architectural project that did stand out from the rest with regard to addressing a greater range of complexity was Hargreaves and Associates' Parque de Tejo e Trancao, in Lisbon. Here, water treatment facilities and landfills are merged with new public park programs, ranging from wetland education and river walks to equestrian pursuits and ball sports. There is a creative attempt in this design to integrate some of the seemingly "dirty" activities of urban infrastructure with recreational and sculptural programs. A striking terrain of overlapping events and adjacencies is made all the more palpable through sinuous earthforms and plantings that resemble more a field topology than a geometry of objects.

Clearly, it is not at all easy these days for a landscape architect to have access to and win over the forces that shape so much of contemporary development, but perhaps this is due as much to the profession's inability to grasp the complexity of our rapidly globalizing culture as it is to the perceived ignorance or arrogance of those same forces. But even for those with eyes to see, the next difficulty involves how exactly one may participate in all of this complexity. So many of our techniques of conceptualization and representation seem inadequate to the task of recharting the landscape project in today's world. New insights into the critical, the tactile, and the complex will most likely follow from innovations with regard to design methods, techniques such as grafting, layering, scoring, and folding. The day that our modes of design generation become less reliant upon solely plan and perspective representation and become more inclusive of temporal and synesthetic techniques will be the day when we can move beyond the current impasse.

In this regard, I believe it is absolutely appropriate to insist upon a landscape architecture that is nothing less than culturally ambitious, nothing less than virulent in its evolving of cultural life. The critical, the tactile, and the complex are three possible paths along which the discipline may advance its visibility and efficacy in cultural affairs. Together with issues of representation and new design techniques, they outline a landscape architecture that may function as a powerful shaping agent in the various metaphysical and political programs that operate in a given society. Here, landscape is not limited to the workings of a strictly external domain, the territory of the scenic ecosystem, beautiful, efficient, and perhaps self-sustaining, but is further extended as a cultural instrument, a lively, inventive, and imaginative player in the development of cultural ideas.

Gardens

Urban Garden. Linda Pollak Architect

38

Gloucester Residence. Child Associates

Grand Isle Residence. Child Associates

Plastic Garden. Dean Cardasis and Associates

Grid and Dimension. Ron Herman Landscape Architect

Murmuring Flow. A.E. Bye, Janis Hall

Unfurlings. A.E. Bye, Janis Hall

Private Residence. Raymond Jungles, Debra Yates

Isgur Residence. Jack Chandler and Associates

The 1234 Garden. Chip Sullivan

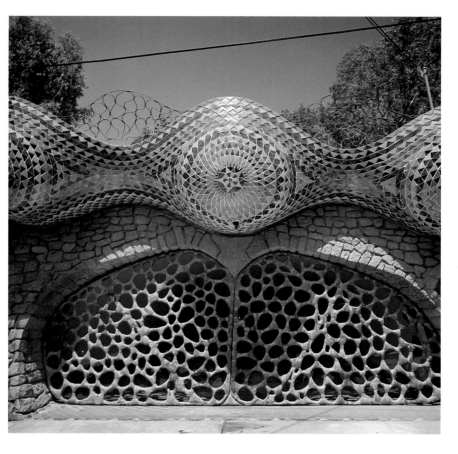

Mexican Whale. Javier Senosiain Aguilar, Espacio Integral

Green House. Javier Senosiain Aguilar, Espacio Integral

Private Residence. Rios Associates

49

Garden Perspectives without Vanishing Points. Ruey Y. Chen

Miraflores. Ron Wigginton/Land Studio

51

Floating Stone Garden. Suzanne Biaggi, Rik Barr

Garden Geray. Bernd Krüger, Hubert Möhrle

Greenberg Residence. Mia Lehrer, Scott Sebastian

Land Art

55

Newgate 1986-1987. David Ireland

Boiling, Balance, Window into Another World, Beyond Fairway. Tanya Preminger

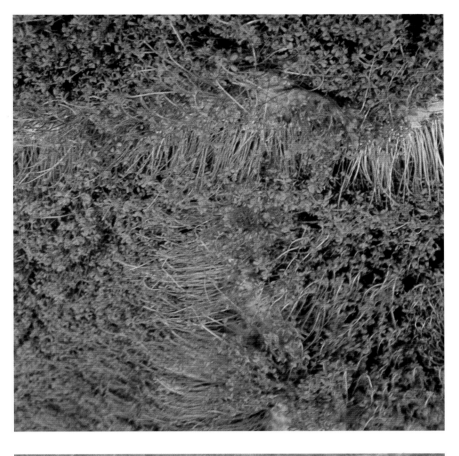

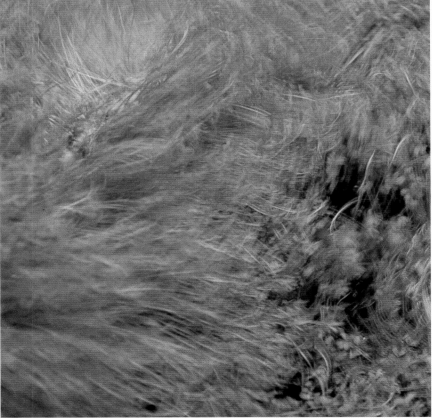

Habitat II. Suzy Hug-Levy

African Burial Ground Memorial. Jeanine Centuori, Karen Bermann

Three Squares. CUBUS Architects

Parking Performance. Heath Schenker

Traversing Reverse Rivers. Mara Adamitz Scrupe

Light Passageway. Anna Valentina Murch, Austin Tao & Associates, Bob Banashek

62

Mother Ditch. B.J. Krivanek, Heidi Duckler, Robert Fernandez

Island Culture. Wellington Reiter

Touch. Jeffrey Schiff

Park up a Building. Vito Acconci & Studio

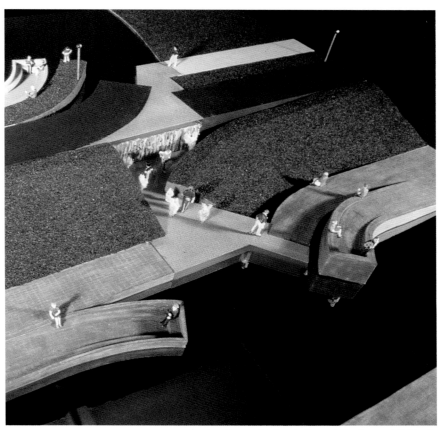

Laakhaven/Hollands Spoor. Vito Acconci & Studio

Flying Park. Vito Acconci & Studio

Grift Park. Vito Acconci & Studio

Mnemonic River. A.E. Bye, Janis Hall

Abundance & Scarcity. Fernanda D'Agostino

Parks

Village of Yorkville Park. Ken Smith, Schwartz, Smith, Meyer

Belvedere Park. Child Associates

Japanese American Historical Plaza. Murase Associates

South Cove Park. Child Associates

Charleston Waterfront Park. Sasaki Associates

North Shore Esplanade Extension. Johansson & Walcavage

Collins Circle, Murase Associates

Naganuma Community Park. Yoji Sasaki, Ohtori Consultants

Naganuma Community Park. Yoji Sasaki, Ohtori Consultants

78

Kreitman Square, Ben Gurion University. Shlomo Aronson

Gabriel Sherover Promenade. Shlomo Aronson

80   **Preservation and
      Reclamation**

Albert Promenade. Tichnun Nof

82

Hotel Explora, en Patagonia. Germán del Sol, Architect

Hotel Explora, en Patagonia. Germán del Sol, Architect

84

Oceanside Water Pollution Control Plant. Royston Hanamoto Alley & Abey

Xochimilco Natural Park. Mario Schjetnan, Jose Luis Pérez, Grupo de Diseño Urbano

Shop Creek Stream Restoration. Wenk Associates

Waterworks Garden. Lorna Jordan, Jones & Jones

Gate Tower Building Roof Garden Plaza. Makoto Naborisaka, David Buck, Nikken Sekkei

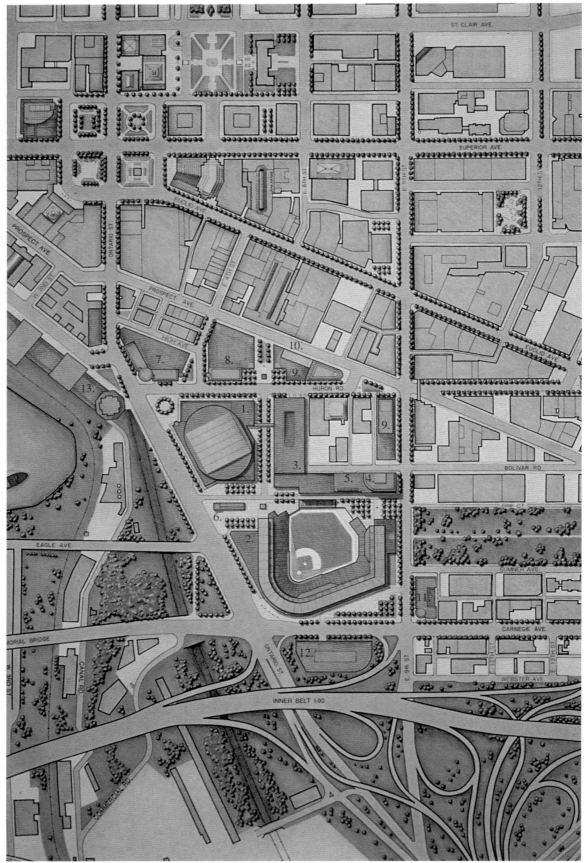

Cleveland Gateway. Sasaki Associates

Cleveland Gateway. Sasaki Associates

Neve Zedek Plaza, Susan Delal Center. Shlomo Aronson

93

Marugame Plaza. Peter Walker William Johnson and Partners

94

Saigon South Master Plan. Skidmore, Owings & Merrill

Santa Monica Civic Center Specific Plan. Roma Design Group

96

Santa Monica Beach Improvement. Wallace Roberts & Todd

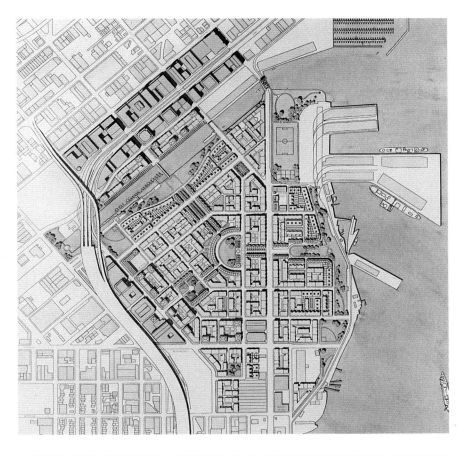

RENDERINGS BY NORM KONDY

Mission Bay Master Plan. Skidmore, Owings & Merrill

Institutions

Therapeutic Garden for Children. Douglas Reed Landscape Architecture

Tsukuba Institute of SANDOZ. Toru Mitani, Sasaki Environment Design Office

Tsukuba Institute of SANDOZ. Toru Mitani, Sasaki Environment Design Office

Wind Hill Crematory and Funeral Hall. Toru Mitani, Sasaki Environment Design Office

Houston Police Officers Memorial. The Office of James Burnett

104

Burnaby Metrotown Civic Center. The SWA Group

The Wood and the Cemetery of the Souls. Iñaki Albisu Aparicio

Center for Contemporary Graphic Art. The SWA Group

TOM FOX

Port of Seattle Pier 69. Murase Associates

Museo de las Culturas del Norte. Mario Schjetnan, Jose Luis Pérez, Grupo de Diseño Urbano

Rancho la Puerta Spa. Chris Drayer Landscape Architect

110

Koga City Folk Museum Garden. Shodo Suzuki

Koga City Folk Museum Garden. Shodo Suzuki

The Neurosciences Institute. Burton Associates

Library Walk. Peter Walker William Johnson and Partners

Center for Advanced Science and Technology. Peter Walker William Johnson and Partners

Center for Advanced Science and Technology. Peter Walker William Johnson and Partners

Kempinski Hotel. Peter Walker William Johnson and Partners

Courtyard for the German Institute of Standards. Richard Weller with Muller, Knippschild, Wehberg

Green Pia Tsunan Central Garden. Yoshiki Toda

Green Pia Tsunan Central Garden. Yoshiki Toda

Osaka City University Media Center Plaza. Makoto Naborisaka, David Buck, Nikken Sekkei

Osaka City University Media Center. Makoto Naborisaka, David Buck, Nikken Sekkei

Corporations

123

Oyama Training Center. Peter Walker William Johnson and Partners

HIKO MITANI

YKK Research and Development Center. Toru Mitani, Sasaki Environment Design Office

YKK Research and Development Center. Toru Mitani, Sasaki Environment Design Office

Great West Life Corporate Garden. Civitas

American College Testing Corporate Campus. Herbert Lewis Kruse Blunck Architecture

Hewlett Packard Roseville Campus. The SWA Group

TOM FOX

Federal Reserve Bank, Dallas. The SWA Group

130

The Gardens and Shops at the Arizona Center. ELS Associates, The SWA Group

131

MacArthur Court. The SWA Group

132

Solana. Peter Walker William Johnson and Partners

Solana. Peter Walker William Johnson and Partners

134

Plaza Tower. Peter Walker William Johnson and Partners

Over the last four decades, pressure from both social and economic forces has radically reconditioned the character of the design professions. Designers now stress the breadth of their services, the inclusive grasp of their practice. This structural metamorphosis has been relatively rapid and conclusive, with large corporate offices emerging from the shaky foundations of the small studio practice. Both the organization and the goals of the profession have evolved to meet new challenges, many of them concerning clients, economics, and implementation, as well as modes of practice.[1]

More in parallel than a direct result, landscape design as an esthetic project closely allied with advanced ideas in painting and sculpture fell into disrepute in the years following the social upheavals of the late 1960s. At the community scale, citizen participation in the decision-making process attacked the authority of the designer or planning commission and sought to temper economic gain with civic well-being. The architecture profession broadened its services, embracing the exterior as well as interior realms. Impulses from seemingly unrelated disciplines and pressures to address a broader range of needs also influenced the way in which buildings were conceived and executed. In landscape architecture, the real threat to the planet as a whole and the "discovery" of ecology as a mediating procedure turned the profession from its historical course: creating exterior settings of vegetal and inert material that understood natural conditions and patterns of human use. Ian McHarg's doomsday pronouncements in *Design with Nature* were instrumental in redirecting the attention of landscape architects from the esthetic accomplishments of design—their cultural and intellectual aspirations—toward a greater understanding of our position in the environment, both negative and positive.[2]

Analysis replaced formal consideration, as if the process by which landscapes were directed, if not created, could result from study alone.[3] As in any era, the resulting designs were of varying quality. The broadened landscape vision, however, was accompanied by a diminution in the design's strength as perceivable space and form.

Then came the backlash. In the 1980s, a new generation of landscape architects saw in distant history a long story of accomplishment and beauty. Almost in one fell swoop, many of the lessons of the Ecological Age were lost, and designers instead turned for inspiration to artists and their works in the landscape.

This was a loaded view, however, since art—unlike design—begins with constraints internal to the artist. In contrast, design remains a social practice (some might say, social art) that needs to consider far broader parameters. To be viable landscape architecture must consider more than form or light quality alone, although this limited range of address is quite acceptable in the artwork. In this sense, artists can serve as the research wing of landscape architecture; design demonstrates applied development. It is true that a number of landscape architects have been rewarded for being artists, and one can rightly develop definitions of practice that cross over traditional lines. A landscape architect can act like an artist, and an artist can assume the manner of a designer; categorizations depend on the approach and the project. But what is the role of landscape architecture in a world continually losing an active engagement with the physical environment?[4] In its place we seek a virtual reality, perhaps as an escape from, perhaps as an enrichment of, the world in which we actually dwell.

The work submitted to the Design Landscape Forum spanned a broad range of types and tread along stray, if well-trodden, paths. To attempt to ascertain clear affinities and directions from the group is very much like comparing apples and eggs. The work we panelists reviewed ranged from festive retail landscapes, to the private world of the residential garden, to the corporate campus, to the public park, to wannabe artworks. Only in their use of vegetation, and perhaps in the shaping of the ground plane, did they display common traits.

Some asserted that ecological process must determine a naturalistic guise. Others suggested that to be a 1980s or 1990s landscape meant striking back with a vengeance at that accepted image of nature. Using patterns and order, they again brought nature under control, suspending the landscape in an eternal instant circa 1989.[5]

The issue seems to be familiar. And although we would all prefer to lay to rest the question of the so-called informal versus formal orders, I'm afraid that stylistically the submitted projects clearly exemplified that very dichotomy. One group of designs appears to have left behind any hint of geometry for nature's greener pastures. Some appeared to advance nature as a model; others suggested that a constructed order, reflective of the human mind, is the proper way to go.

Despite a great variety of particular idioms, some more natural, some more obviously treated as pattern or sculpture, landscape architecture at the end of the twentieth century seems to be falling into two major divisions. One group rejects any sense of identifiable form, exchanging that urge for the look of nature. The second group rejects its forms, if not its systemic performance, for an overt human expression. This is the old formal/informal grouping once again—the formalist designs smack of hubris, and while skilled as formal manipulation, beg the question of ecological reason: plants fill out a shape or occupy a pattern, and monospecies set out in great number seem to be tempting fate. The naturalistic approach is hardly less problematic. We inhabit landscapes, defined by J.B. Jackson as the product of human dwelling interacting with the land. But land is no longer natural; innocence ended with habitation. Thus, the problem becomes determining what nature is, and what it directs. As the Dutch landscape historian Erik de Jong has stated, "there is no such thing as nature in the singular." It is not that simple; there are many natures. Our conception of nature is dependent on the historical and social context.[6]

Nor is there any simple or single application of factors perceived as being natural. Given that the projects submitted to the Forum were experienced only in color slides and explained with limited accompanying written explanations, it is hardly any surprise that evaluation was based primarily on the design's formal aspects. Of course, this is problematic, reducing landscape architecture to a visual phenomenon, discarding any appeal to the other human senses or to task. Nor were the submissions, for the most part, coherent or comprehensive. Few provided any sense of the immediate or greater context, and how the design fit as a piece of a greater entity.

Designers' claims notwithstanding, it was virtually impossible to accept, for example, the ecological performance of certain land reclamations, or to dismiss more formally conceived landscapes as being antisocial or inappropriate to their sites. How much can the "look" of the landscape tell us about its validity and performance? Must an ecologically conceived design look natural? If so, why? If the program calls for human recreation, the landscape is no longer functioning as it was in its natural state. What are viable forms for complex programs that interweave considerations of ecology, human activity, form and space, and horticulture? Are there strategies that appear more promising in generating landscape architecture for our times?

Within the intersections of these stray and wandering paths loomed another large question: Where does the human occupant enter into these designs? Remarkably few slides included people. The sole exceptions to this dearth of human presence seemed to issue from the more corporate landscape design offices, whose images smacked of the developer's promotional brochure in which everyone plays or shops happily together. We should not forget that even the most formal of garden and landscape designs constitutes a setting for people. Spiro Kostof, in his monumental history of world architecture, reminds us that architecture is inextricably bound in both "settings" and "rituals"—both the place and the event.[7]

We must also consider the seemingly more mundane matters of maintenance and control. As early as the 1950s, Garrett Eckbo raised the question of maintenance in garden design, acknowledging that many people today have neither the time, nor the means, nor the desire for extensive upkeep.[8] In Eckbo's work, this consideration, paired with considerations of areas of more intense use, often led to more paving than planting.

Most of the designs reviewed for this Forum, however, appeared to avoid the issue of care, implying that the state of the landscape is eternal, or that intense gardening was a desirable practice, which, of course, it may be for certain projects. But landscapes grow or die. Change is inherent in all living systems, and in turn, becomes a key ingredient in landscape—as opposed to architectural—design. Few schemes addressed either growth or change; nor was there much to suggest the power of time to inform the history of the landscape. Why this avoidance of change? Must we always choose between process-oriented landscape design, which never seems to appear as tidy artifact, and the tidy design, which never seems to address process? The merging of the two directions suggests fertile terrain for making landscapes in coming years.

For the immediate future, we could formulate two plausible directions. The first continues the notion of a formally ordered landscape, perhaps drawing on architectural or sculptural ideas, perhaps more accepting of environmental management practices. Rather than a reliance on a monospecies planting that courts ecological disaster, or a design that demands the continued use of the spade and the shears, let us suggest one in which the vegetation is allowed to take its course. Here, more in the Japanese manner of mixed formalities, the intersection of two orders—human and horticultural—can create a landscape of more than one dimension.[9]

The second approach looks more deeply into the ecological processes, and sees within them the suggestion of form that geometry or an artificial construct borrowed from the art world would never have invented. Beyond merely addressing the logic of drainage, erosion, growth, sunlight, and orientation, prevailing breezes, and horticultural suitability, one may find in them the generators of landscape form. The resulting esthetic derives not simply from analysis, but analysis and understanding translated to form. If, in the past, we have used the shape, color, and texture of a single plant as the basis of planting design (think of the monochromy of the White Garden at Sissinghurst, or more generally, the planting of rose gardens), we would now look at the systemic workings of these ecological systems as instigators of the perceived world, used by designers not as a free-for-all, but as a landscape esthetically and socially conceived.

Early applications of this approach already exist. In Gilles Clement's *jardin en mouevement* in one area of the Parc Andre-Citroën in Paris, the seeds of grasses and wildflowers were sown without any exact preconception of the form they would take over time.[10] In an accelerated Darwinian evolution, the microclimatic and localized forces coerce an initial and constantly changing garden within the formal structure of the park as a whole. It is a daring experiment in which the designer, like a coach, must be content to establish the parameters and then let the participants take charge.[11]

Waterfront park developments by Hargreaves Associates in Louisville and Lisbon harness the coercive force of flowing water to derive planning at the macroscale and more particular, localized landforms in accord with social activity.[12] In these cases, the designers have abrogated the idea of simply creating a naturalistic scene; instead, we enter a zone of managed hyper reality in which all the players appear familiar and yet the forms they take are novel. As more than one participant in the symposium stated, a landscape doesn't have to look natural to be E.C. (Ecologically Correct).

Why try to recreate a nature that is today nostalgic and out of step with current patterns of use? We can't recreate Yosemite. Can we instead imagine landscapes that will develop from a deeper understanding of natural systems and our position within them? New uses, new trials, and new factors will determine the look of fabricated natures in the future. There is every indication that they will be designed and managed, whether as acts of preservation, creation, or interpretation.

137

Notes

1 There is a danger in this shift, however, as sociologist Robert Gutman has pointed out. Traditionally, a professional serves as an instrument for both the individual client and the public good. As the image of the design professional becomes more closely associated only with the desires of the client, the public's respect for the profession wanes. See Robert Gutman, *Architectural Practice: A Critical View*. (New York: Princeton Architectural Press, 1988).

2 Ian McHarg, *Design with Nature* (Garden City, New York: Doubleday, 1966).

3 I have discussed this trend at greater length in "Form, Reform (and American Landscape Architecture)," in *Het Landschap/The Landscape* (Antwerp: deSingel, 1995), pp. 37-52.

4 See Michael Benedikt, *For An Architecture of Reality* (New York: Lumen Books, 1987), and

Marc Treib, "An Island in the Riptide toward Dissolution," *Journal of Architectural Education,* Volume 40, Number 2, Jubilee (1987): pp. 78-79.

5 See Marc Treib, "The Place of Pattern," *Pages Passages*, Number 4 (1992) pp. 128-134.

6 Erik de Jong, "Nature in Demand: On the Importance of Ecology and Landscape Architecture," *Archis* (October 1996): p. 65.

7 Spiro Kostof, *A History of Architecture: Settings and Rituals* (New York: Oxford University Press, 1985).

8 Garrett Eckbo, *The Art of Home Landscaping* (New York: McGrawHill, 1956), especially pp. 238-245.

9 The mixture, or embeddings, of ordering systems is inherent to historical Japanese design. See Marc Treib, "Modes of Formality: The Distilled Complexity of Japanese Design," *Landscape Journal* (Spring 1993).

10 Gilles Clement, *Le jardin en mouvement: de la vallée au Parc Andre-Citroën* (Paris: Sens & Tonka, 1994)

11 Depending on one's tastes, this piece of the park may or may not be judged as successful. At certain times of year, for example, its hodgepodge of plantings more closely resemble those of a vacant lot than a garden. We must bear in mind, however, that the "garden in movement" is but one "wild" segment (like the *bosco selvatico* of the Italian Renaissance garden) of a highly mannered French landscape. Thus, this miniature meadow is normally read as controlled, if not always visually ordered.

12 See "Hargreaves: Landscape Works," *Process Architecture, 128* (1996).

Urban Garden
New York, New York
Linda Pollak Architect

This 39th floor terrace occupies the top level of an aluminum-clad volume of a 1980s mixed-used tower designed by James Stewart Polshek. The client's apartment overlooks the terrace from the two penthouse levels of a stone-clad component of the building. Because of its unusual location, the project had to negotiate significant technical constraints, including wind uplift, the inability to tie any new construction to the existing building, and the need to accommodate unwieldy window-washing equipment.

An assemblage of constructed ground planes of stone and grass corresponds to the edges of the terrace and their disparate conditions of exposure. The terrace's identity is constructed in relation to view, and boundary is figured as physical and visual connection to city, river, park, and building. Stainless steel channels planted with grass provide an armature for the installation of slate paving slabs in three different widths. Stainless steel planter boxes contain flowers or grass.

At the west edge of the terrace, a fountain forms a threshold between the library and garden. Slate stepping stones traverse this fountain, where seven water jets offer a constant gentle sound. The fountain is designed to complement a similarly dimensioned rectangular planter wall, which incorporates four bronze panels and two layers of planter boxes.

ELLIOT KAUFMAN, LINDA POLLAK

Gloucester Residence
Gloucester, Massachusetts
Child Associates

This vacation house garden for a couple who love to entertain sits on a tiny sliver of land—1/16th of an acre—on Rocky Neck Harbor in Gloucester, Massachusetts. From the small shingled cottage, exposed and crowded by neighbors, extend parallel shingle walls the length of the garden on either side from the house to the water's edge. These walls create both an inner private garden and a viewshed to the great harbor beyond.

From a small lower dining terrace by the house, one looks through the frame of a pergola across the lawn terrace, bordered on each side by splayed drifts of seaside perennials, and out to a spectacular view of Rocky Neck Harbor.

The garden includes *Clematis paniculata* framing the dining terrace, and *Vitex, Perovskia, Buddleia, Potentilla, Rosa rugosa*, and honey locust trees planted to reinforce the architectural elements that frame the vista to the sea. This garden is a room with a view—a small contained inner world of lawn infinitely expanding to the sea and the horizon.

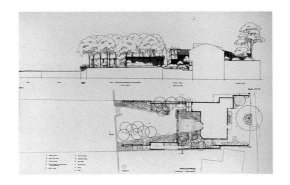

© FELICE FRANKEL

Grand Isle Residence

Grand Isle, Vermont
Child Associates

This 80-acre site is located on a high peninsula on Grand Isle, overlooking Lake Champlain. The property is composed of a beautiful natural diversity of land forms and vegetation: a headland of shale cliff forested with white cedar, a slope of beech woodland, a wetland of birch and maple, a cove edge of beach and grasses, and a high, wide meadow. The ground cover throughout is fragile, diverse, and rich, consisting of blueberry, partridgeberry, and fern.

To unite the diverse parts of the property into a single design, we devised a scheme of the least intervention possible. The garden is a system of viewing platforms, boardwalks, steps, and pavilions that loosely join the house to the outer reaches of the property.

In the craftsmanship of its wood joinery and the intimate relationship of its garden structures to the surrounding nature, the built elements of the garden recall both nearby Adirondack lodges and Japanese traditions of woodland retreats.

There is no precise definition of beginning or end to the garden's itinerary. A boardwalk floats above the fragile wetland like an island without a beginning or an end, enticing visitors to explore the natural landscape beyond.

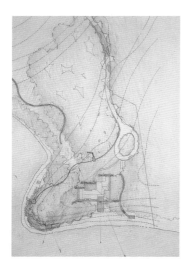

Dream of the Sea Ranch
A 56-minute documentary film
Zara Muren

Sea Ranch is already recognized as a work of classic significance, remarkable for its environmentally sensitive design. *Dream of the Sea Ranch* captures this development in history. Begun in the 1960s, the "dream" was that residential development could not only be designed to fit the land, but could also be planned to incorporate landscape restoration and to enhance the natural beauty of the site. This fine and compelling purpose is seen in the work of the design team at the 10-mile-long coastal site in Northern California. On-camera interviews with landscape architect Lawrence Halprin, and architects Joseph Esherick and the late Charles Moore are interspersed with shots of their models and drawings and sequences showing their realized schemes. The documentary goes on to explore how the reality has diverged from the dream over the last 20 years in the face of political and economic pressures. The documentary was funded in part by a grant from the National Endowment for the Arts.

The Landscape Architecture of Roberto Burle Marx
A 57-minute documentary film
Zara Muren

Roberto Burle Marx's death in 1994 closed a richly innovative chapter in Modern design. This film is a living record of the work and ideas of the great Brazilian visionary over a career spanning 50 years. Through interviews with Burle Marx, his humanist values and artistic aspirations are exposed, setting a framework for understanding his work. The film explores a diverse selection of 11 projects including Copacabana Promenade, IBM, Itarmarity Palace, and the Monteiro residence. The photography captures the lyrical and dynamic quality of Burle Marx's compositions, and also their living reality as humanized, managed landscapes. In the final sequence, Burle Marx takes us to his home, garden, and, nursery—site of his most daring design experiments and some of his most perfectly realized work. The documentary was funded in part by a grant from the National Endowment for the Arts.

Plastic Garden
Northampton, Massachusetts
Dean Cardasis and Associates

Much recent experimentation in landscape design has focused on the garden as idea—metaphor, symbol, image—and neglected the spatial experience of people who will enter the garden. This work, though energized by contemporary site-specific ideas and materials, is ultimately about landscape space, articulated and sudivided into useful and inspiring volumes that take on meaning as people occupy them. Here, Plexiglas, wood, and gravel are combined with the vinyl-sided house, plants, and morning light to create a distinct landscape space.

Except for the animation provided by numerous children, the client's neighborhood was depressing and spiritless: a utilitarian subdivision in which an existing forest had been clear-cut to uniform depth behind each equally setback house on each half-acre lot. The client's house, completely clad in vinyl with few windows or doors, was conceived with no regard to its site and sat upon the open land like an abandoned plastic toy. The concept for the plastic garden was to bring the razed woodlot to the house, hollowing out of it three irregular descending terraced spaces flowing from the interior spaces of the dwelling. These gardens would reach out from the plastic house with playful, light-transforming, plastic panels designed to engage the plants, stone, and wood. The result is that the static patterns of the neighborhood are interrupted and counterpointed by the garden's complex and playful spatial geometry, and a funny kind of balance is achieved between the plastic house and its site. The garden creates an intriguing entrance by juxtaposing transparent, translucent, and opaque colored panels with the existing woodland, morning light, new deck, and gravel terrace.

In the plastic garden, one enters a wacky, colored origami. The experience unfolds within the garden, redefining the outer context of woods, subdivision, and sky by coloring, blocking, and silhouetting them, and forming an inspirational and functional spatial experience for the family and the children who play here.

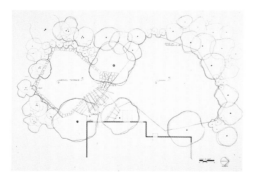

Grid and Dimension

San Francisco, California
Ron Herman Landscape Architect

This garden provides a strong focus for the entry, circulation, and living spaces of a house in Pacific Heights. This garden is a minimalist reference to a checkerboard garden of moss and stone in a Zen temple in Kyoto, Japan, and was designed for a client who greatly admires Japanese traditional gardens.

Bronze metal is employed to achieve a precise grid, echoing the Zen garden. The grid becomes three-dimensional in the northeast corner of the courtyard, which drops in elevation, and a pond at the south end of the courtyard is raised in elevation from the grid. In the white south wall is a stainless steel door leading to the garage, a service access for the court-yard. A freestanding glass wall intersects the bronze-edged pool and acts as a shoji screen. Water flows over the edge of the pond, creating the constant sound of a rushing stream.

Three plant materials are used in the garden: moss, mondo grass and bamboo. The bamboo provides foliage, recalls Japan, and offers a sculptural presence against a large bare wall of an adjoining residence.

By incorporating a multiplicity of reflective surfaces, the designer has endeavored to give an ethereal quality to the garden. Crispness of line and detail are intended to give the garden a sense of elegance.

Murmuring Flow
Southwestern Connecticut
A.E. Bye, Janis Hall

In an area of southwestern Connecticut characterized by rolling hills, rock outcroppings, streams, and ponds, this landscape and site-specific sculpture for an 8-acre residential parcel containing a red brick Georgian house introduces flowing streams to a site that was surprisingly dry for this region. An old walled garden at one end of the house had been filled with high-maintenance flower beds that were thoroughly overgrown, their geometric plan only faintly visible.

A visitor now follows the flow of spreading yew planted along the front of the house toward the garden gate, and, upon entering, is greeted by boulders and fieldstone. Though unexpect-

ed, these stones seem to belong to the site, and they redefine the scale of the garden. No water actually flows here, but two converging streams are implied by the placement of the stones, which continue for about 300 feet behind the houses, and the yew, which is planted in a 150-foot-long stretch at the front.

As Murmuring Flow moves along, it engages the terrace, the lawn, and sweeping spruce branches. The sculpture approaches a woods, which responds to it with a long, light-filled space cut into the trees. From inside the house, individual segments of the piece become part of each room as the house extends along the crest of the hill and the length of the sculpture.

Unfurlings
Eastern Pennsylvania
A.E. Bye, Janis Hall

For a 25-acre parcel on what was once a 250-acre farm, sculptor Janis Hall began by paring down to the site's essentials, which required removal of crumbling concrete walls, decorative fish ponds, exotic plants, and an unusable swimming pool. A hill rising behind the house and rolling down around it to the street dominated the scene. After sculpting the earth in large, bold moves, the designer created an animated, undulating hill that unfurls from the top, establishing in its wake serpentine walls, a pool, seating areas, plantings, and the client's house.

Three lengths of curving stone walls engage the hill into which the house is nestled, separate an existing tennis court, and define the pool area. Trees punctuate the flowing earth and serpentine walls, casting significant shadows. The pool is nestled into the hill, wrapped by curving stone walls and a weeping beech hedge stretching 150 feet. The pool area is an island within the unfurling flow of earth, walls, and trees.

The site is now connected to the larger view of contoured farm fields reaching out into the distance beyond.

144

© JANIS HALL

Private Residence

Miami, Forida
Raymond Jungles, landscape architect
Debra Yates, mural artist

Raymond Jungles and Debra Yates wanted to create a garden that highlighted her paintings and his landscape designs. An existing pool was resurfaced to give it the look of a lagoon and to make it highly reflective during the day. A regularly shaped pool deck was cut into a more organic shape and made smaller. This strategy allowed meandering pathways and interesting patios to be inserted around and adjacent to the pool deck. The garden was heavily planted so that a natural, almost overgrown, garden was the result, reminding its owners of visits to the jungles of Brazil.

The designers introduced plants for interior arrangements, to attract butterflies, and produce fragrances. Awnings, paint, and the introduction of a sculptural bougainvillea trellis impart a strong visual image, individualizing an otherwise common residence. Art, predominant in the interior spaces, reappears in the garden, unifying indoors and outdoors.

Jungles met Roberto Burle Marx in 1979. Beginning in 1982, he visited Burle Marx at least once a year, traveling with Burle Marx on working trips and plant collecting expeditions. Yates began painting on exterior walls, much as Burle Marx created abstract paintings in his gardens as tile mosaics. Most of Yates' paintings are very large, so they are a natural for gardens. She installs her work from scale drawings, and materials are hand selected by the artist as part of the design process.

Isgur Residence

Woodside, California
Jack Chandler and Associates

On a large corner lot, this garden was designed as a dramatic outdoor room for entertaining and showcasing the clients' outdoor art collection. The house, originally a typical ranch style home, was renovated by the architect Mark Mack, who inserted a bright orange cube in the center of the house.

The design plays off the abstract, cubist nature of the remodeled house, picking up the color and strong horizontal lines of the structure, while juxtaposing vertical elements with the horizontal.

Formerly a walnut orchard, the front yard now focuses on a fountain, which begins as three bubbling jets at the base of an orange wall. The water flows out and down the terraces in a rill that culminates at a 4-foot-deep round echo chamber, which amplifies the

sound of the falling water. The fountain can be heard in the master bedroom upstairs, masking the sound of passing traffic. Adjacent terraces are planted with olives, lavender, gauva, blood grass, and fountain grass.

A fountain serves as a new focal point in the rear yard as well. It begins close to the house, beside a new pergola. In a pool flanked by a low, stepped wall is a 3-foot-square granite block, split in half; water is piped up through the split and into the pool, from where it spills under the pergola into two channels. These channels reunite and flow 100 feet across a lawn of stepped terraces into a 6-foot pool. Shade tolerant plants, including azaleas, ferns, and Japanese anemone, were installed under existing trees; ornamental grasses and perennials dominated other areas. Herbs are planted close to the kitchen, and a rose garden lies behind a gridded screen fence.

The 1234 Garden
Berkeley, California
Chip Sullivan

This garden is laid out along a main axis that bisects the center of a 1923 craftsman bungalow house and terminates with a trellis that frames a trompe l'oeil of the garden in perspective. This device is based on the false perspectives fashioned by Borromini in the Palazzo Spada in Rome. Because the garden is so small, a variety of such illusionistic devices are incorporated: the spine of the garden breaks apart into smaller asymmetrical spaces, created by a series of parterres filled with colored gravel. Glass gazing globes are arranged to distort reflections. From his studio seat, the designer can look out on these glass globes and see the garden reflected in many different ways as the light changes throughout the day. At either side of the central trompe l'oeil are secondary forced perspectives, terminated with mirrors. When viewed from the studio and specific points in the garden, they create the illusion of a much larger setting. Cypress trees are arranged to enhance the central axis, and the garden is brought to life through the use of sweeping interconnected lines, patterns, and brilliant color contrasts.

Mexican Whale
Javier Senosiain Aguilar,
Espacio Integral

The concept for this house is man's search for his natural space, his historical roots, his cultural and building traditions, and harmony with nature. The stonework facade is reminiscent of the pre-Hispanic past. A polychromed cladding of pieces of ceramic tile was applied to the exterior to create the image of a whale emerging from the sea. The concept evokes the most characteristic features of pre-Hispanic architecture: strong volumes and color. Private and guest areas are defined by an embryonic form and separated by a hallway that creates an open and centralized space similar to an Arabic patio.

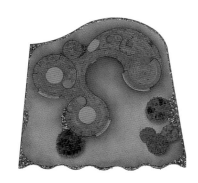

146

Green House

Javier Senosiain Aguilar,
Espacio Integral

The concept for this house was to create two spaces, one very bright with plenty of light in order to cook, eat, and play; the other is designed to be darker, more enclosed, for night—to read and relax. The two rooms are linked by a narrow tunnel. The house, which faces south, is partially buried and can hardly be seen from the exterior. A visitor encounters only green grass dunes with trees and plants, inviting rest and meditation. To walk in the garden is to walk over the roof without even noticing.

Garden Perspectives without Vanishing Points

Santa Ana, California
Ruey Y. Chen

The idea is to suggest a larger world within the context of a limited site, and to design with entropy. By allowing ready-made imperfections to exist naturally, disorder and order coexist in the garden without hostility. The two-way relationship of the view coming in and the garden reaching out is the key strategy for successful integration. The inner garden's contribution to the scheme also suggests a broader imaginary context.

Angled walls create perspectives without vanishing points, giving the illusion of indefinite depth. The gentle turbulence of a water wall further enhances the movement and sound of a pond.

Juniper crawls across a white trapezoidal planter, horizontally extending the garden vista to the far west yard.

From the top of the stairs flows a green lawn that seeps from under a neighboring wall, erodes a path through the stairs, and collects in a grassy mound at the center of the garden. The dynamic and irregular design takes the static lawn and creates the illusion of a moving stream.

147

Private Residence
Southern California
Rios Associates

The site for this 2.11-acre residential project, located in a south-facing canyon in the mountains of Southern California, included challenging utility easements, dramatic topography, and a long and narrow lot configuration. These characteristics were catalysts for the design of the project, which attempts to develop outdoor spaces that frame and enhance the owners' collection of contemporary sculpture.

Traditional elements of the garden are exaggerated, including the edge band, perennial garden, crushed stone path, and stone wall. These features take their skewed geometry from the site, and their supernatural scale is emphasized by long views and the elegant simplicity of their palette.

The house itself emerges from a terraced "lake" that begins at a loggia at the building's ground floor. A thin line of water drops over each terrace, falling finally into a crushed stone pathway on the lowest terrace level. The water is then recirculated through the crushed stone of the walkway using a specially designed biological filtration system.

Stairs to the east of the lake open to the lawn and a Richard Serra sculpture of curved steel plates. A swimming pool at the western edge of the lawn is tucked against terraces and a natural rock outcropping. On the west side of the lake, crushed stone pathways border gardens that echo agrarian themes and hug the steep slope. At the top of the slope, low stone walls create precincts for citrus trees, herb beds, and greenhouses.

Landscape architecture is charged with the task of creating art that is habitable, where both concept and function are valued and neither is compromised. This project explores the relationship between architecture, art, and landscape architecture, expanding the options of appropriate roles, forms, and materials for each.

PHOTOGRAPHS BY D. VORILLON

Miraflores

Fairbanks Ranch, California
Ron Wigginton/Land Studio

Our site design, program, and bands of plant and tree species at Miraflores represent a geographical description of San Diego's beach-to-mountains ecological scheme—palms to suburban lawn to forest. Land Studio's intent was to compose a scenario for this speculative residence that represented Southern California's fascination with its own image.

We sited the house at the rear of the property to create a grand entry experience. Beginning from the street, the entry sequence establishes a sense of grand expectation: a distant house, a grand drive, a forest drive-through, and a great lawn leading to the house, with its porte cochere and library. We placed

a double allée of tall *Washingtonia* palms to identify the front door and continue beyond the back, pinning the house to the landscape.

A dense forest of randomly spaced alders was planted across the property. This dark forest canopy sets up a dazzling, open view as one emerges at the house. The forest was also designed to conceal overflow guest parking; guests find their way to the house along a grass "stream."

Behind the house, the requisite Southern California swimming pool and spa follow the oblique angle of the library and porte cochere at the front of the house, a strategy that allowed a longer pool. A subtropical landscape links the house to an existing eucalyptus grove.

Floating Stone Garden

San Francisco, California
Suzanne Biaggi, sculpture court
Rik Barr, garden design

This garden creates a contemplative respite from the frenetic energy of its urban setting. The small backyard garden has as its focal point a granite sculpture court. The stones bear witness to the passage of time by the patina of moss and lichen that they acquired in a quarry abandoned more than 80 years ago. The serenity of this area is enhanced by the sound of water quietly splashing into a pool that holds fish and aquatic plants. In contrast to the monochromatic courtyard, pathways lead through a garden of rare and unusual plants to a granite bench placed for garden viewing. The lawn creates the feeling of a lake, cool and quiet.

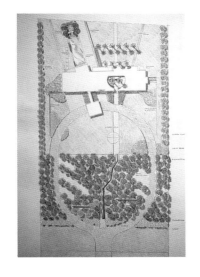

Garden Geray

Hohenlohe, Germany
Bernd Krüger, Hubert Möhrle

This private residence is situated in southwestern Germany in a hilly landscape with vineyards, old castles, and historic palaces. The site is the estate of Schönau, which was built in 1780 but has been altered and extended many times. According to historical records, the estate belonged to Duke Ludwig Friedrich Carl of the Holy Roman Empire and Duke of Hohenlohe-Neuenstein, who bequeathed it to his mayor and land manager Friedrich Wilhelm Carl of Imhoff.

The present owner, a friend of the family, put a lot of effort into the quality and contemporary design of the garden which picks up on and reinterprets its historic links. The main design concept is to avoid small elements in the main courtyard and the other building areas, thereby enhancing the generous and expansive proportions of the complex.

Different seating areas are scattered around the garden, which create various experiences in relation to the house and the landscape. Very important was the opening of the garden to the surrounding landscape by removing a large pine hedge, thus establishing a new frame for the surrounding agricultural fields of sunflower, sweet corn, and grains. The seasonal change intensifies the garden experience.

Natural stone is used to differentiate areas. Baroque beds with *Buxus* hedges, *Taxus*, and roses are hidden in some small garden areas, which include an herb garden and a fish pond.

Greenberg Residence

Los Angeles, California
Mia Lehrer, Scott Sebastian

The clients had lived for many years in a 1930s-era house on a large wooded lot. They decided to tear down their old home and build a much more extensive residence suitable for entertaining and for the display of their art collection. They did not, however, want to lose their mature landscape, especially the many large trees that had been growing on the site for up to 60 years. This presented a difficult problem as the new house would not only fill a major part of the lot but would also require extensive regrading.

The solution was a landscape design that involved two distinct phases of construction. First, during the grading operations the largest of the trees were relocated. These included mature coral trees, jacarandas, dracaenas, and palms up to 80 feet in height. Some of the trees were replanted within a few feet of the stakes and strings that indicated the future walls of the house. All were carefully positioned, as if they were sculptures, to have specific relationships to the views from the future windows, terraces, and balconies. The rest of the plant material was boxed and stored on the site during the nearly two years of construction.

The architectural vocabulary of the house, designed by Mexican architect Ricardo Legorreta, relies on large space-defining walls. The landscape architects proposed additional walls that extend out from the house to create outdoor rooms of various scales. Some were built of block and stucco; others became hedges. The rooms were furnished very differently: the arrivals court is a desert with only a cluster of palms on the entry axis and a mass of agaves against one wall. Along one side of the house, the service access winds through an informal meadow. At the rear, turf extends down to the pool in four perfectly level steps. Along the bedroom wing is a series of secret gardens: one for roses, one for camellias, and a cutting garden with a variety of flowers.

Newgate 1986-87

San Francisco, California
David Ireland

"Ireland has ventured out-of-doors in public commissions, including New-gate 1986-87, located at Candlestick Point on the San Francisco Bay, in a former refuse site that is being revital-ized into a state park and recreation area. Intrigued by the bleak disorder of the environment, Ireland created an im-posing sculptural landscape that draws it cues from the immediate surround-ings. Reconfiguring the massive rubble of concrete slabs and rebar that litters the grounds, he constructed two mega-lithic walls that gradually converge into a narrow passageway leading to an un-compromised vista of the bay. Rising from the desolate chaos that surrounds it, Newgate poses a primeval grandeur that recalls its namesake, Newgrange, a stone age burial ground in Ireland made of more than 4,000 tons of rock." Karen Tsujimoto

"Ireland's walls relate to and inter-act with the human body and experi-ence, as well as with the physical envi-ronments in which they are placed or for which they are created. Some are inviting, even luring, and can be walked into. Many speak of social his-tory or existing social situations, or make historical and art historical refer-ence, often with elements of irony and pun. All change the space around them significantly and often the space of the entire gallery or space they exist in. Almost all deal with light in some way. And the issues of materials, move-ment, density and what I continue to think of as 'Ireland air' (the empty space in and around his works that holds and reflects light and narrative) are, of course, key to much of Ireland's work." Leah Levy

Boiling, Balance, Window into Another World, Beyond Fairway
Shfaim, Israel
Tanya Preminger

These four projects by Israeli artist Tanya Preminger date from 1989 to 1996. Preminger works with natural materials in various art media, including sculpture, landscape art, installation, and photography, She has had 16 one-woman exhibitions in Israel as well as 41 group exhibitions in Israel, Russia, Korea, Japan, the United States, and five European countries.

Regarding these works, which use soil, grass, mirror, basalt, and black marble, Preminger relates, "Everyone expresses themselves through themselves, their place and time. My materials are between earth and atmosphere. My ideas are between seriousness and laughter. My place is between West and East. My time is between past and future."

Habitat II
Istanbul, Turkey
Suzy Hug-Levy

Men have always asked themselves where they come from, who they were, and what they are going to become. Considering that people throughout the world have been and are still today being, for various reasons, either forced or choose to quit their homelands, it appears that our century has been the century of exiles and deportations. Habitat II developed from this concept.

The work consisted of three pieces—a video, a carpet, and a statue installed on a path covered with earth. The carpet, made out of lentils grown on cotton and plastic, was placed between the video of a performance there and a root-headed statue. Man takes root, longing for his other self and the land he was forced to leave.

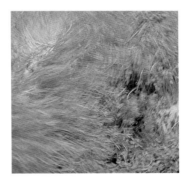

African Burial Ground Memorial

New York, New York

Jeanine Centuori, Karen Bermann
assistants: John Hollo, F. W. Weak

This design won first place in the African Burial Ground Memorial Competition to commemorate the unmarked and forgotten burial ground of 18th century Africans and African Americans that emerged in the course of excavation for the construction of a federal office tower in lower Manhattan.

The traditional African grave site is "an animate charm," a window allowing communication between the living and the dead. Ancestors and descendants, history and possibility, meet at the surface of the ground. This proposal transforms all the existing concrete sidewalks on the site, replacing them with new sidewalk panels made of concrete and other media contributed by many members of the New York community—artists, writers, neighborhood organizations, school children, and others.

Each panel will have embedded in its concrete surface decorative and symbolic objects, fragments, and text which honor the spirits of the dead and communicate elements of the African-American experience in the tradition of the West African gravesite, urban graffiti, and the quilt. Existing metal curb trim will receive metal plates bearing the names of participants. Manhole covers will be replaced with covers bearing the legend, "The African Burial Ground—Walking among African Graves—Speaking through the Ground."

Three Squares

Bergen, Norway

Arne Saelen, CUBUS Architects

In a recently designed street in Bergen, custom design detailing is illustrated in paving, walls, and granite toppings, curbs to fit the needs of wheelchairs and trolleys, manholes, tree grilles, benches, and sculpture.

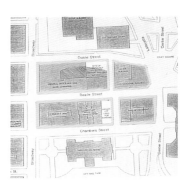

Parking Performance
Sacramento, California
Heath Schenker

Landscape architects constantly do battle with the automobile, which dictates so much of the configuration of the urban and nonurban environment. The most common approach to parking lot design is to camouflage cars, but Parking Performance, which was held March 1, 1987, tackled the nemesis, working with it rather than against it, making use of the fact that cars aren't anonymous but are driven by people.

The idea was to park a large number of cars in an empty lot in a prearranged pattern according to color, and then to play a musical composition for car horns, transforming cars into a visual composition and instruments in a musical performance. The car-horn score, entitled "Toot Suite," comprised first and second movements recalling rhythmic dance variations. The improvisational third movement recalled weddings, New Year's Eves, and traffic jams.

The cars were arranged in a grid pattern arranged at about 30 degrees to that of the large university parking lot where the performance occurred. This pattern, which echoed urban streets and agricultural fields, was designed to be highly visible from the air, making Parking Performance an art form of the future visible from space. But the goal of the work was to produce in viewers a double take, a second look, a focusing on the juxtaposition of this particular pattern and behavior with what one normally expects from the automobile.

Traversing Reverse Rivers

Annandale-on-Hudson, NY
Mara Adamitz Scrupe

Traversing Reverse Rivers, a site-specific temporary project, was created on the campus of Bard College in Annandale-on-Hudson, New York, during the summer of 1995. Composed of 1,000 plastic emergency water storage bags, concealed electrical wiring and 7-watt lights with photocells, the piece measured approximately 300 feet long by 40 feet wide and was installed along an abandoned roadbed, in partial view of the Hudson River. The water storage bags were filled with water pumped from the Hudson River, and then hauled several miles to the site. Before the bags were arranged, the lighting components were designed and installed along the site.

Light Passageway

St. Louis, Missouri
Anna Valentina Murch, artist
Austin Tao Associates, landscape architect
Bob Banashek, electrical engineer

Light Passageway is a sequence of lightscapes and shadowboxes that illuminate the fabric and terrain of St. Louis's Metro Link light rail system. After the train leaves the station, passengers glimpse a "garden light well" to the south. Sunlight filters through a high canopy of existing trees to light an understory of native flowering trees, shrubs, and ferns that have been introduced to make a lush green ground plane. To the north, passengers view parking garages screened with two layers of stainless steel mesh, creating a shimmering moiré pattern.

The train then moves through a narrow, dark, walled passageway cut by four openings. Like frames in a movie, these doorways reveal colored light washing the back walls and utility pipes along the tunnel's north side. After passing through a tunnel, the passengers see another "garden light well." Here, a diagonal line of support columns flocked with glass beads marks the crisp edge of a planted landscape and the beginning of an amber-to-red shattered glass landscape on the south side; a luminous field of blue glass lies to the north. Red tones on one side and blue tones on the other suggest the Doppler effect to viewers moving through them.

This hardscape incorporates 160,000 pounds of discarded colored art glass (which is not normally recycled) and energy-efficient lighting to create a crystalline landscape. The journey through "Light Passageway" ends with a view of the original limestone-walled tunnel glowing beside the dark garnet and iridescent blue glass.

Mother Ditch

Los Angeles, California
B.J. Krivanek, artist
Heidi Duckler, choreographer
Robert Fernandez, composer

The Los Angeles River, once deeply connected to the city's lifeblood, is now reduced to the status of big ditch. Channelized and completely entombed in concrete, it winds through culturally diverse residential and industrial zones of the city.

At a riverside site in the Atwater Village neighborhood, "Mother Ditch" was a multidisciplinary performance designed to create a narrative of an overlooked neighborhood, incorporating movement, sound, visuals, and text and evoking the river as a metaphor. Just as the river has been tamed into invisibility, the vast melting pot of Los Angeles assimilates all comers— Mexican, Japanese, Armenian. Yet these diverse communities persist, refusing cultural entombment.

Exploring the link between the river (water flows) and immigration (people flows), visual artist B.J. Krivanek, choreographer Heidi Duckler, and composer Bob Fernandez transformed the river site into a twilight spectacle. Working with dancers, a rock climber, riverfront residents, a contingent of Gabrielino Indians, a violinist in a boat, an interdenominational choir, and various local groups, including the Harley Davidson Club of Glendale and Dave's Accordion School, the collaborators orchestrated eclectic movements and sounds within an evening landscape dominated by projected text that symbolized the hieroglyphics of a lost civilization. The event suggested the polarization of nostalgic memory and contemporary urban reality.

Seeing Around

Halifax, Nova Scotia
Andrea Wollensak

Wollensak, a New York-based artist visiting the Nova Scotia College of Art and Design, mounted seven welded-iron box frames on the walls of the Anna Leonowens Gallery in Halifax. Each supported two holographic plates containing images of human skeletal sections and text. These plates, layered 5 inches apart, produced a visually disconcerting effect as the viewer peered through the first holographic image to find a second three-dimensional representation floating behind it. On the floor, small clusters of government-issue aerial photographs of Halifax were placed under short stacks of half-inch-thick plate glass. The historic battlements of the Citadel, a Halifax landmark; naval dockyards; and an airforce base featured prominently in these aerial surveys. Suspended on silk threads above the images were pulley-mounted brass plumb bobs, counter-balanced so that viewers could raise and lower them easily. These marking devices hovered in the space as strategic projectiles which, if severed from the fragile silk threads, would drop and damage the glass, metaphorically attacking the images of military installations below.

Wollensak plays upon the "esthetics of disappearance," as subtle shifts in one's gaze render the holographic images invisible; the aerial photography component reflects the military-industrial context of Halifax's economy. She constructs a predigital, nonelectronic environment that force a viewer to locate the physical point of access to each piece. One must stand directly above the aerial photographs to fully view their amplified images through the thicknesses of glass, and shift one's gaze back and forth to observe both layers of holographic images as they phase through each other, hauntingly revealing the three-dimensional images of the human skeleton.—Peter Dykhuis, *C Magazine*

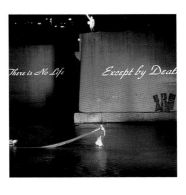

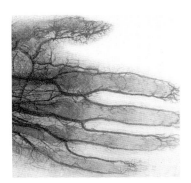

Island Culture—
A Sculptural Investigation
of Isolation and Containment
Boston, Massachusetts
Wellington Reiter

Islands have always been magic—their "otherness" being a source of intrigue, fantasy, and romance. Frequently the site of events that would not be possible, required, or permitted on the mainland, islands possess an autonomy that has provided inspiration for numerous artists and writers. The Boston Harbor Islands are characterized by all of the above and, while rarely seen, these satellites have been essential to the development of the city.

In museological terms, pedestals are essentially man-made islands, their purpose being to isolate objects in space from the distraction of the surrounding environment. Not incidentally, the pedestal also bestows a cultural status that serves to separate art from the everyday. But while pedestals cele-brate culture, islands are often used to put out of sight that which society would prefer to ignore. Again, Boston's islands are no different, and the structures built on them frequently speak to our society's fears, biases, and desire for control.

Consistent with previous projects by the artist, Island Culture brings issues of the natural and built environment into the gallery and translates them into a language that responds to the unique characteristics of the space. While based on real history and geography, the essential focus of the project is to suggest that common themes operate at both the art and urban scale. For example, Island Culture would seem to confirm two Brancusian notions: 1) that sculpture will find a new standard in the work of the engineer (a new sewage treatment plant on Deer Island in Boston Harbor, for example, recalls giant eggs) and 2) the pedestal is never a neutral armature.

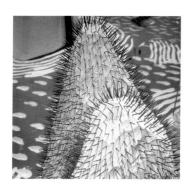

Touch

Katonah, New York

Jeffrey Schiff

This project, installed in the garden at the Katonah Museum of Art, creates a ritual surrounding touch, rarefying the moment of contact between viewer and environment. Touch consists of a platform built above a gravel ground and around a towering pine, upon which are organized the necessary props and devices for a ritualized experience of touch. The project centers on two distinct experiences: the sole of the left foot touching the gravel ground, and the sole of the right foot touching the trunk of the tree. In the first instance, the viewer, after removing left shoe and

sock and placing them in the designated box, steps over to the structure to the left. The left hand grasps a rail, the right foot steps up to a stop, and the bare left foot steps through a hole to the gravel below. As the left foot descends, the right hand is placed in a bowl to feel gravel from the site that has tumbled until smooth. To enact the right foot experience, the bare foot is gently rubbed against the smooth stone dome; the viewer then relaxes on the padded platform. Grasping the handles with both hands and pulling, the viewer propels the wheeled platform forward, so that the right foot passes through an opening in the wall that masks the tree trunk, and comes into direct contact with the tree bark.

Two projects that lift the land up into the air:

Luis Vera, Jenny Schrider,
Charles Doherty
Vito Acconci & Studio

Park Up a Building

Santiago de Compostela, Spain

In Spain, Alvaro Siza's Centro Gallege de Arte Contemporanea, was the site of this temporary installation in 1996. Two types of park modules are suspended from the side of a building. One park module comprises a metal floor with seats on opposite sides; the other is a floor with a seat on one side, a tree—its roots still in its burlapped ball—on the other. A light from beneath each floor illuminates the park. A connecting step joins one module to another, and each successive module is hung one step higher than the one preceding it. As a visitor tours the park, he or she climbs the side of the building. The park adapts to buildings of different heights.

Two projects that mix land and water:

Luis Vera, Jenny Schrider,
Charles Doherty
Vito Acconci & Studio

Laakhaven/Hollands Spoor

The Hague, The Netherlands

In the preliminary proposal for Laakhaven/Hollands Spoor, The Hague, a waterfront development incorporates a U-shaped channel that runs through a university campus, offices, stores, and private residences. Animated public spaces are proposed to help define the development as a new city center.

The land drifts out into water, while water slips in through the land like a ship in a stormy sea. Half a landmass is cut away, and pivoted out into the water; each successive half of land is halved again, and pivoted out in turn into water. (Where continuous passage is needed, the gaps between land are covered with grating.) As the land shifts out, it also shifts up or down, sinking under water or creating a waterfall over a retaining wall.

Flying Park

Dayton, Ohio

This proposed southern gateway to downtown Dayton, birthplace of the Wright Brothers, is conceived as a monument to flight. A steel grating ramps up the center of a traffic island and, supported by steel trusses, passes over trolley lines on each side of the street. The structure resembles the wings and tail of an airplane, and supports a park, accessed by concrete stairs from the sidewalks below. Walkways around the perimeter of the wings and tail surround a raised garden of ground cover, trees, and seats, lit from within. At the end of each wing is a blinking light; from underneath, a mist sprays the structure so that it appears to float on a cloud. Below, a line of lights, like those on an airport runway, line the strip.

Grift Park

Utrecht, The Netherlands

In the proposal for Grift Park in Utrecht, the Grift River meets an elevated pond. At the exchange point between different water levels, as if the land can't bear the collision, the land "explodes." On top of the slope, the paths separate. A waterfall flows down onto the lower level. Grating over the water allows passage from one end of a pathway to another. A visitor can walk between sprays of water, lit at night from underneath the grating. Below, the slope breaks off and sinks as it curves out toward the river, pushing the walkway with it.

Mnemonic River
Massachusetts
A.E. Bye, Janis Hall

At Mnemonic River, earth, air, and water become nearly indistinguishable and dream, contemplation, and experience become interchangeable.

The initial design move was to cut a sweeping, riverine edge between the meadow and the lawn, suggesting an image of the meadow as a riverbank and the lawn, a river. Plants were massed in islands providing further ambiguity of water and earth.

The earth behind the house is in the form of a gentle, dry riverbed evoking a visual echo of the bay, which often heaves and flows in shapes similar to the land and engages the background of Great Hill. Light and shadow play are revealed on the undulating earth and the surface of the bay.
Clockwise: Spring afternoon, autumn morning, autumn evening winter morning

Abundance and Scarcity
Marylhurst, Oregon
Fernanda D'Agostino

Abundance and Scarcity is an investigation and meditation on food—the growing of food as a crop, the coming together around food at meal times, and our diverse cultural attitudes toward food. It is a statement about food as an intimate link between people and nature. Through food, we are tied to the land and its seasons and to the whims of the weather. Food is also one of our most universally understood ties to each other as people. Though most of us have not recognized it, hunger is also something we recognize and dread.

The designer's grandmothers were women of the Depression who made a life's work and art out of feeding people. The memory of their creativity with food, both as cooks and as people who managed to get others fed, was one inspiration for this piece. Others were the fields of corn, cribs, granaries, and haylofts in which the designer played as a child in Pennsylvania. She sought to recreate the physical joy of walking in the corn or through grain on a threshing floor. This piece, with its grown crop, the granary, and its paths marked by proverbs, may call forth from viewers their own thoughts and memories about food and the land.

Charleston Waterfront Park

Charleston, South Carolina
Sasaki Associates

The primary goal was to create a public open space as the first step in the redevelopment of the city's waterfront. The street grid was extended with pedestrian ways to and through the park to link Charleston's historic residential and commercial districts with the river.

A gravel promenade parallels the river's edge, connecting the main park entrance to the north with a residential community to the south. The promenade is enhanced by traditional Charleston benches and a low seat wall, a continuous row of palmettos, and decorative lighting integrated with the railing design. The raised seat walls define a simple lawn.

A bronze and cast stone pineapple fountain, symbolizing Charleston's hospitality, forms the centerpiece of the lawn. Along the urban edge of the park, a more protected, intimate quality is created by four rows of live oaks that shade walkways, seating areas, and eight small gardens.

A fishing pier terminates the Vendue Wharf, which aligns with the main park entrance. Bluestone-paved Vendue Plaza forms the principal park entry and connects all the park elements. Another fountain on axis with Queen and Vendue Streets serves as a beacon to the many people who live in and visit downtown Charleston.

Belvedere Park

New York City, New York
Child Associates, landscape architects
Mitchell/Giurgola, architects
Martin Puryear, sculptor

The site is located on 1.6 acres at the northwestern corner of North Cove on the Hudson River in the commercial heart of Battery Park City, New York. Belvedere Park is both a gateway to Wall Street and a park for the North Cove community, thus providing a harbor entrance to lower Manhattan for New Jersey ferry commuters, a place of repose for the public amidst the vibrant activity and immense architecture of the World Financial Center.

The principal design elements of Belvedere Park include a majestic bosquet of high canopy oaks, arranged in a grid on a plane of peastone across the upper level of the site; a serpentine battered granite wall pierced by open-

ings to the lower level at the river's edge; and a raised circular belvedere that provides a viewing platform to the Statue of Liberty and the sea beyond.

The park provides a link between the geometric, minimalist plaza that fronts Cesar Pelli's World Financial Center and the curvilinear Romantic park to the north. Its bosquet is an esthetic response to Pelli's gridded fenestration at the World Financial Center. The serpentine granite wall that supports the bosquet suggests the curving lines of the park to the north.

The esplanade, edged with informal groves of honey locust, wraps around the site at a lower level along the Hudson River. A magnificent broad sweep of steps descends from the upper level of the bosquet to the river and is marked on either side by 60-foot sculptured pylons—a gateway to the city at the water's edge.

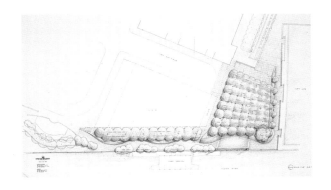

Japanese American Historical Plaza

Portland, Oregon
Murase Associates

The Historical Plaza was conceived as a memorial to acknowledge the tragedy of the internment of over 110,000 Japanese-American citizens during World War II. To the east, the "dragon" gateway and wall are composed of rough-hewn basalt that curls along the Willamette River. To the west, the "tiger" gateway is marked with two bronze sculptural columns that describe in relief the history of Japanese Americans from the early Issei immigration to the present. To the north is the "tortoise" gate, where a large stone is set in a low earthen mound recalling the legend of islands where immortals are supported on the backs of giant turtles. The south entry is perceived as the legendary phoenix, where the story of the Japanese Americans begins.

Large granite stones symbolize the Japanese immigrants coming to Oregon; like the evolving Japanese community, the stones gradually become a wall, solid and whole. A break in the wall symbolizes how the Japanese-American community is broken with evacuation and relocation during the war. The large standing stone in the center of the plaza is engraved with the names of the 10 relocation camps, and the paving stones surrounding them are fractured, reflecting broken lives and shattered dreams.

Barnsdall Hollywood Tower and North Corner Park

Hollywood, California
Lehrer Architects

The Barnsdall Hollywood Tower and North Corner Park are born out of a new master plan for Frank Lloyd Wright's Barnsdall Park, completed with Peter Walker William Johnson & Partners in 1995. The tower and park serve as a monumental terminus to Hollywood Boulevard to the west and an extension of the pedestrian precinct of Los Feliz to the north. With a ticket center, information kiosk, and food concession, the tower and park take a critical and amorphous place in the city and complete and connect it to Wright's 1920s park, the only Wright-designed landscape that is in use as a civic park today.

North Corner Park was created by eliminating a minor street between Hollywood Boulevard and Vermont Avenue, transforming a leftover triangle into a significant parcel. This strategy significantly calms traffic and solves the parcel's awkward geometry. As monument and signage, the Barnsdall Hollywood Tower will announce North Corner Park as a major gateway to Barnsdall Park, as it was in Wright's original scheme.

BRUCE FORSTER

BRUCE FORSTER

TIMOTHY HURSLEY

South Cove

New York City, New York
Child Associates, landscape architects
Stanton Eckstut, architect
Mary Miss, artist

South Cove, a 30-acre park, is located at the southernmost tip of Manhattan Island on the 92-acre spectacular artificial landfill site of Battery Park City. Behind South Cove, the World Trade Center rises to awesome heights. Across the water lies the Statue of Liberty and the Atlantic Ocean. Nowhere in New York is the confrontation between the city's man-made elements and its natural setting more dramatic than at South Cove. The Battery Park City Authority commissioned a collaborative team of artist, architect, and landscape architect to provide a refuge for a new low-rise residential community from the awesome architectural and environmental forces surrounding the site.

The design concept emerged from the study of natural coves and mari-time structures along the North Atlantic Coast. From these, the landscape designer abstracted generic elements of all coves and created a prototypical cove—a metaphor for the park.

Drifts of native, coastal vegetation, a dunelike topography, and a rock-strewn "inner shore" of South Cove evoke the natural coastal condition of protected coves. Densely planted meandering groves of multistem locust, sweeps of beach grass, and beach rose counter the linear seawall and the harsh built maritime environment. The spacing of wooden piles in the water and the placement of the trees in the grove express the substructure of beams and piers that supports the park. Upper walkways and lower promenade merge and meander along the cove's edge, inviting exploration of the jetty and giving visitors a variety of vistas of the waterfront and the Statue of Liberty. The planting, wood structures, lowered pathways, rocks, steps, and lights are designed to draw visitors to the water's edge.

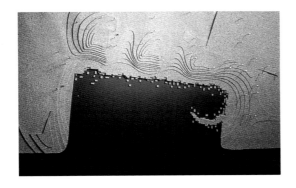

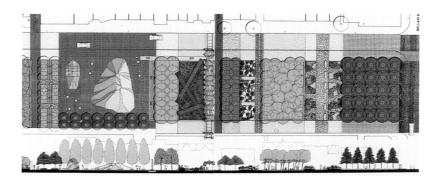

Village of Yorkville Park
Toronto, Ontario
Ken Smith, landscape architect
Schwartz, Smith, Meyer

This park is the result of an international competition launched by the city of Toronto in 1991. The competition called for a new park to establish a foothold for nature in the city and create an oasis in an urban area less than an acre in size, sited above a subway station. The design accomplishes all this in a demonstration of urban ecology, education, local history, and regional identity.

The idea for a park for the Village of Yorkville dates back to the late 1950s, after the Victorian rowhouses on the south side of Cumberland Street were cleared to make way for Toronto's subway system. Local residents fought for a park to be built over the subway. Instead, a parking lot was created, but residents continued to press for a park until the city finally agreed in 1973. It took two more decades before the new park was designed and built.

The park's design reflects the history of the Village of Yorkville and the diversity of the Canadian landscape. Our objective was to reflect, reinforce, and extend the scale and character of the original village, while providing unique inner-city ecological opportunities for the introduction and display of native plant species and communities. We also sought to provide a variety of spatial and sensory experiences, landscape qualities, and park functions, and to link the park to existing pedestrian walkways and adjacent areas.

To achieve these objectives, the park was conceived as a series of gardens that vary in width, their frames symbolic of the lot lines of the rowhouses that once stood on the site. Each garden contains a distinct collection of plant communities ranging from upland conifers and deciduous species at the east end of the park; lowland and wetland communities and a granite outcrop in the central portion; and shade gardens at the west end. The largest element is a 700-ton rock outcropping that was moved 150 miles and reconstructed as the site's sculptural centerpiece.

The park transforms the idea of the Victorian collection box into a collection box of Canadian landscapes arranged along the lot lines of the former rowhouses. The result of these influences is a contemporary variation on the traditional garden, one that gives new readings to traditional concepts of nature in the city.

North Shore Esplanade Extension
Staten Island, New York
Johansson & Walcavage

This waterfront project links the Staten Island Ferry terminal in downtown St. George, Staten Island, to a 6-mile walkway at the water's edge in New York Harbor. The goal of the Economic Development Corporation of New York City, which funded the project, was to stimulate the economy of Staten Island by encouraging the many visitors and tourists using the ferry to stop and visit this prime waterfront property.

The recently completed project includes a pedestrian walkway created by widening the bus ramp from the ferry terminal. An important way station along this walkway is a tensile pergola designed by FTL Associates. This graceful structure defines a stopping point for an excellent view of the harbor.

Beyond the tensile structure, the path curves back inland to frame the elegant, golden yellow Bridge and Tower by Siah Armajani, whose personal philosophy of democracy in public space design was an important contribution to the spirit of the project.

At the top of the tower is a light, and incorporated into the design of the tower's steel structure is a silhouette of a house. With these two elements, the tower represents a lighthouse. Descending through the tower, one is drawn down into the site and into a long alley flanked by trees, authentic marine buoy moorings, and historic stone and brick buildings.

One arrives at a large public plaza bordering the harbor, where complex paving patterns are seen in non-traditional color combinations. Site furniture is arranged in random groupings rather than more formal arrangements to emphasize how people socialize.

Collins Circle
Portland, Oregon
Murase Associates

Collins Circle is a traffic circle on the edge of inner-city Portland, and has been an important landmark to residents for many years. A light rail station is to be built nearby with trains passing Collins Circle, which has been redesigned to serve as a gateway to the city. A large abstract stone sculpture, representing the neighborhood's rebirth, is composed of basalt from the Columbia River Basin. The stone parallels burial mounds and prehistoric megaliths, the stone gardens of Japan, and the volcanic activity that shaped the Pacific Northwest.

Enclosing the stones are eight transplanted young oak trees that were uprooted from nearby streets for the light rail construction. Sumac trees and

upright stones erupt out of the circle to accentuate it and give it presence. The circle, a primordial symbol, traditionally means a place of gathering, of coming together, and of healing, but this island is only for visual use. Brush completely encloses the base to discourage foot and wheel traffic, since the rock feature is not meant for climbing. The sloping circle, angled toward the sweeping curve of the light-rail tracks and punctuated with standing stones and three gnarled sumac trees, is open to many interpretations, and signifies the resurgence of nature. As the train turns in the street, viewers will behold changing views with variable light conditions. Although the visual experience at the circle may be short, the images are designed to linger and engender many opportunities for reflection.

Weesner Family Amphitheater

Apple Valley, Minnesota
HGA Landscape
Architecture Group

The Weesner Family Amphitheater at the Minnesota Zoo was designed to accommodate birds of prey shows and has also become the site for a growing number of outdoor concerts. The amphitheater and its support building take advantage of lakeside topography. Rather than camouflaging the ensemble as a strict imitation of natural forms, the designers chose to emphasize the amphitheater's connection to nature through contemporary materials that suggest the wings of soaring and gliding birds. In an unusual approach, the landscape architect considered not only the zoo, but the birds themselves

as its clients. It sought to create humane living conditions for these avian stars while incorporating streamlined building systems that celebrate their beauty for the audience.

Visitors enter at the base of the amphitheater and ascend the hillside when leaving. A small introductory space exudes the precision of a parterre in a formal garden. Continuing on, visitors encounter the rocky forms of a holding barn, which forms a backdrop to the stage set and symbolizes glacial outcroppings that evoke the region's ecological history.

The theater's location allows for diverse staging possibilities in future bird shows. Pole-mounted cages were placed at the far edges of the lake so that the birds can make a dramatic entry at the beginning of the show.

Betty Marcus Park

Dallas, Texas
Sasaki Associates

Betty Marcus Park, built in conjunction with the Myerson Symphony Center in the heart of the Dallas Arts District, provides an outdoor extension of the center's cafeteria and a setting for the display of contemporary and Classical works of art. The informal garden design is a counterpoint to formally planted Flora Street, the Arts District's pedestrian-oriented main thoroughfare.

The large glazed lobby of the Myerson Center forms the north edge of the south-facing site, dramatically increasing the amount of light and heat directed into the park. It was important that the park design mitigate the noise

of Pearl Street, a busy street that runs along the south side of the park. A water wall screens the traffic noise, and the park is designed to be more formal adjacent to the Myerson Center, and more informal and heavily planted toward Flora and Pearl Streets.

To provide much-needed shade for the outdoor café, the designers specified large trees and large umbrella tables. Herbs, which are incorporated in special dishes by the café chef, are planted adjacent to the terrace and glazed lobby wall. This simply detailed space is a place to exhibit small-scale works of art, have a meal or snack, enjoy an outdoor intermission, and meet performers after a concert.

Naganuma Community Park
Naganuma, Japan
Yoji Sasaki, Ohtori Consultants

Naganuma Community Park is located 30 minutes by car from Chitose Airport in Hokkaido, in the middle of broad pastureland and fields at the foot of the Maoi Mountains in the town of Naganuma. This park is based on a proposal for a 1989 design competition and is intended to promote the utilization of thermal energy and the development of recreational functions on a regional scale. It is centered on the town-administered Naganuma Hot Spring Community Center, which is used by local residents.

The first project to be realized was Maoi Auto Land, a suburban "auto camp," which has been laid out to integrate the facility with the surrounding pastoral landscape. Each camp site is open to the landscape, as the result of a zigzag arrangement, and the buildings blend with the greenery. The facilities are unified by three basic colors. Fragments in primary colors respond to one another, yet maintain a slightly tense relationship. The intention was to create a device that stimulates communication with nature.

Water Park, the next facility to open, is a stage on the water that has as its backdrop the evening landscape of Hokkaido. The park is intended to be the point of connection between visitors and nature, which in this area possesses a grand scale.

Kreitman Square,
Ben Gurion University

Beer Sheva, Israel
Shlomo Aronson

Kreitman Square is designed to communicate the tension between the organic flow of a desert landscape and the formal rationality of a campus environment. This duality is expressed by integrating several design features including a desert stream, an arcade, mounds, lawn, and desert trees. The final result is a public meeting place that projects a symbiosis between nature and the man-made.

Gabriel Sherover Promenade

Jerusalem, Israel
Shlomo Aronson

The Gabriel Sherover Promenade overlooks one of the most majestic and emotional views in the world: the Holy City of Jerusalem. The architectural challenge for the design was to create an urban environment and promenade within a desert landscape.

The design includes a range of elaborate details: pergolas, railings, light fixtures, and drinking fountains. These details were crafted to give the walls and belvederes an elegant appearance set in the edge of the desert. The planting of 800 mature olive trees and wheat fields reinforces the hard spaces and relates to the Kidron Valley below and the descending Judean Hills in the distance.

Piatt Park on Garfield Place

Cincinnati, Ohio
Meyers Schmalenberger Meisner

The design for Piatt Park was part of a study aimed at coordinating an urban design plan, housing redevelopment plan, and phased park/streetscape improvements for the Garfield Housing Development in downtown Cincinnati. This master plan study provided the direction for detailed design of the park, surrounding streetscapes, and public pedestrian areas. It also provided direction to the architectural massing for new buildings proposed for the city housing program. The preparation of this plan was conducted concurrently with an assessment of the market potential for housing development in downtown.

The detailed design for the park retained the strong axial design recommended in the master plan, but revised many of the preliminary site details. The park design concept is based upon the historic axis of the space; a double row of honey locust trees recalls double rows of trees existing in the park since the 1820s. Two historic presidential sculptures are relocated from within the site to either end of the axis. Two new fountains at the center provide focus and transition across an intersection. A central promenade with small sitting spaces extends the length of the park. Perennials line the promenade and provide changing color and interest throughout the year.

The Garfield Plaza at the east end of the site provides the setting for an outdoor cafe for this proposed 1,000-unit housing redevelopment.

vironment. At the heart of the plan lies a visitor center with its geological, botanical, and zoological exhibitions all connected to the promenade along the rim.

Oceanside Water Pollution Control Plant
San Francisco, California
Royston Hanamoto Alley & Abey

This 27-acre secondary treatment facility also provides 6 acres of land for the San Francisco Zoo's Mammal Conservation Center.

Part of the inspiration for the form of the landscape was the geomorphology of a canyon. The 45-foot canyon in which the complex is sited met the dual need of hiding the treatment plant from view, as well as allowing controlled access for trucks, service, employees, and the public. The scale and simplicity of sheer canyon walls fit in with the design philosophy that an industrial esthetic can be inherent to a work of civic landscape architecture.

The sand dunes and coastal vegetation of the adjacent Great Highway, Golden Gate National Recreation Area, and nearby Golden Gate Park also inspired the form of the landscape. The sinuous quality and texture of the dunes and the rhythms of the Pacific Ocean were considered to be part of the surrounding landscape context. At adjacent Fort Funston, weathered, partially buried, massive and obsolete concrete bunkers from past world wars provided a cultural landscape reference for the use of large-scale concrete to provide form for the canyon walls and the two tunnels that connect the canyon to the adjacent roads.

The landscape architects' work included: collaboration on site and zoo planning; design development of outdoor public and employee areas, outdoor furnishings, face of canyon retaining walls and tunnels, and grading of dunes; construction documents for grading, perimeter fencing, planting, and irrigation; and construction review.

174

Xochimilco Natural Park

Mexico City, Mexico
Mario Schjetnan, Jose Luis Pérez,
Grupo de Diseño Urbano

The floating gardens of Xochimilco are the last remnant of the ancient lacustrine life in the Valley of Mexico, and were included by UNESCO in its list of "world inheritance sites" in 1987. Approximately 270 hectares were designated for a multipurpose park. Grupo de Diseño Urbano (GDU) with Mario Schjetnan as partner in charge, created the design of the master plan and specific projects as well as site supervision and coordination. The master plan includes a plant and flower market; a sports park with lagoons and archeological conservation sites; a large lagoon with a landing stage for tourists; and a natural, botanical, and recreational park.

The central area is conceptually a didactic space, with a botanical garden that recreates natural ecosystems found on Mexico's high plateaus and the chinampas, highly productive agricultural islands. A visitors' center includes informative videos, exhibits, souvenir shop, cafeteria, offices, and a computerized information system on the Xochimilco region with ethnographic, botanical, and archeological exhibits.

A recreation area includes a grass esplanade for concerts, picnicking, and promenades along the aquatic and flower gardens. Bicycles, a tourist tram, and launch for boating trips are available. The buildings are integrated into the landscape with berms, terraces, and plants that preserve natural character. The plant and flower market are arranged as a composition of multiple greenhouses, organized around a central plaza and three converging axes.

Parque do Tejo e Trancao

Lisbon, Portugal
Hargreaves Associates

This winning scheme for a 160-acre environmental park supports a wide range of educational and recreational activities, and is spurred by Lisbon's selection as the site for Expo '98. The design seeks to transform a deteriorated site near the Lisbon waterfront, incorporating a wastewater treatment complex into a public park. Recreational facilities include a marina, festival plaza, playing fields, golf course, equestrian facilities, tennis courts, volleyball courts, an amusement park, shops, and cafes.

The sculptural landforms have both a functional and a symbolic rationale. Functionally, the project had to accommodate 500,000 cubic yards of sediment from the dredging of the harbor. The land began to take shape symbolically as a series of arched berms that appear to have been sculpted by the ever-present wind. These metaphoric waves also recall the meeting of wind and water. While the entire park is clearly man-made, the earthworks progress from a more natural expression at the river's edge to clearer manipulations further from the water, suggesting a logical distribution of program. Marshes have been restored to provide wildlife habitat.

An inventive canopy is designed to mitigate the odors of the wastewater treatment facility. The project is not an attempt to heal the damaged site by returning it to to its previous healthy conditions, which would really be little more than a simulation of an extinct landscape. Rather, the site is recycled as a public amenity.

Shop Creek Stream Restoration
Aurora, Colorado
Wenk Associates

Urbanization in the Shop Creek drainage basin had caused severe channel erosion. Downstream, sedimentation and phosphorous pollution had become significant problems in Cherry Creek Reservoir. Most of the channel damage had occurred in visually and ecologically sensitive areas of the Cherry Creek State Recreation Area adjacent to the reservoir.

The solution developed by an engineering team and Wenk Associates is a radical departure from standard landscape architectural and engineering approaches to stream channel design. The project transformed a heavily eroded, unstable stream that was an ecological and esthetic liability to a vital and inviting demonstration of self-sustaining and diverse upland and wetland ecology.

Soil-cement drop structures were designed to help align the channel to visually blend into the prairie landscape. Extensive wetlands were created between the drop structures to mitigate wetlands lost in the construction, and to create significant new areas of wildlife habitat.

The project has received national and state engineering and landscape architecture design awards for its innovative response to the broad range of engineering, esthetic, and ecological issues addressed.

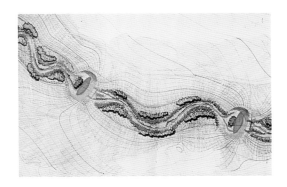

Waterworks Gardens

Renton, Washington
Lorna Jordan, artist
Jones & Jones, landscape architects
Brown & Caldwell, consulting engineers
Fuji Industries, contractors

Waterworks Gardens is a public artwork designed in collaboration with
artist Lorna Jordan. The project is
designed to treat stormwater, enhance
an on-site wetland, create garden
rooms, and establish 8 acres of new
open space for public use. Stormwater
runoff is collected from the grounds of
the wastewater reclamation plant and
pumped into 11 ponds that settle out
contaminants and sediments. Water is
then released into the wetland below,
helping to sustain plants, microorgan-
isms, and wildlife. The stormwater
treatment ponds and the wetland form
an earth/water sculpture that funnels,
captures, and releases water. Within
a setting of native plants, a pathweaves
through the wetland to join trails from
the cities of Renton and Tukwila. Along
the walk, visitors pass though five gardens designed to abstractly express a
large-scale flowering plant.

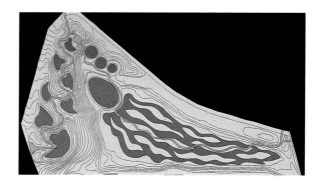

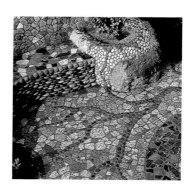

Gate Tower Building
Roof Garden Plaza

Rinku Town, Japan
Makoto Naborisaka, David Buck
Nikken Sekkei

Located in Rinku Town, Japan, a new waterfront reclamation links Osaka with the new Kansai Airport. This roof garden plaza is located 6 meters above ground level over a parking garage. The site measures 70 by 150 meters in area and is accessed directly from the adjacent train station and the Gate Tower Building, a hotel/office complex.

Planned as an events plaza, the design makes extensive use of planting and water to reflect the expansive natural elements of the nearby ocean and mountains. The plaza, when viewed from the building, appears to be floating above the water.

A 5-meter-wide-by-200-meter-long canal with fountains, wooden decking, extensive planting, and benches forms a linear rest space, connecting the northern side of the site to Gate Tower Building and making a visual link to the ocean. A series of low, stepped linear plantings forms the western corner of the plaza, providing a strong visual form viewed from the building and

focusing views, at eye level, back into the main plaza. Within each planting strip is a single species of evergreen. Each one varies slightly in color, texture, form, and flowering period, and is separated by steps of blue tile. Three stone circles provide secondary focal points and allow access to the lower parking levels and street level entrance to the building. The distinctive paving strengthens the sense of rhythm in the design and provides contrast to the calm areas of planting and water. Specially designed cast aluminum benches recalling images of breaking waves are placed to provide accents and places to sit at key locations.

Cleveland Gateway

Cleveland, Ohio
Sasaki Associates

Cleveland Gateway, a new downtown sports district, is part of a well-developed and sophisticated strategy for urban economic revitalization. Gateway was realized with the cooperative efforts of the City Planning Department, Gateway Economic Development Corporation, and two major league sports franchises.

The new sports complex, which includes a baseball park and basketball arena, is carefully positioned to form street edges and urban sidewalks that fit seamlessly with the existing downtown street and block pattern. By depressing the playing surface of each sports facility, their respective ground-level concourses correspond directly to the sidewalk. This strategy avoids the multiple ramps and stairs that commonly surround arenas and ballparks. Entrances to the ballpark and arena are related directly to a sequence of public spaces connected by new streets.

The significant service requirements are combined in a service area underneath Gateway Plaza. To avoid siting the complex within a sea of parking, new and existing parking garages have been constructed and identified to fulfill daytime downtown requirements and night and weekend events at Gateway. Extensive work with the teams and city traffic and parking officials was required to establish location and design standards for 14,000 spaces that were mutually acceptable for shared parking and that satisfied event arrival and departure standards. Gateway is also connected to the regional and local public transit system.

The urban design plan for Gateway is part of a larger economic strategy that locates development of hotel, office, retail, and residential uses on adjacent sites. Along with other projects, Gateway helps establish downtown Cleveland as a vital place in which to work.

Neve Zedek Plaza, Susan Delal Center

Tel Aviv, Israel
Shlomo Aronson

This inner city plaza enhances a new center for dance and theater and a renovation of two historic school buildings. The use of citrus trees as shading devices and channeled water are symbolic of past surroundings which included groves of citrus trees and irrigation channels. Palm trees stand at either end of the Neve Zedek Plaza as markers or gates to the public space. Palms also flank the facades of both performance buildings, reinforcing the perimeter. Particular attention has been paid to surface treatment, especially paving and illumination. The interventions are intended to work together to create an oasis near the center of downtown Tel Aviv.

Marugame Plaza

Marugame, Japan
Peter Walker William Johnson
and Partners

This plaza is the central gathering place near a new museum, library, train station, and mixed-use center. Commuters enter through a series of shops and then ascend via escalators to the train platform. Passengers have a view into the plaza and the central communal court of the town. To the south the museum is situated on a great porch overlooking the train station and plaza.

The design of the plaza pavement comes from two sources: the fabric patterns of Japanese kimonos, and Japan's beautiful civil engineering. This engineering includes the careful way precast pieces of concrete are assembled, and the special asphalt incorporated in sidewalks and streets. The design blends fine materials, including cobbles; the basalt-like slate of the new museum; and the asphalt of the street.

A fountain produces planes of water that offer translucency like a fog or a shoji screen. In recognition of Marugame as a major high-tech container port on the inland sea and along the Takamatsu, the fountain is designed to recall both the gates to the city and the great cranes that lift containers onto the ships.

Saigon South Master Plan

Ho Chi Minh City, Vietnam
Skidmore, Owings & Merrill

Saigon South is a master planned 7,500-hectare expansion for Ho Chi Minh City, Vietnam, to accommodate a projected growth of one million people. The city hopes to manage the physical expansion generated by extensive economic growth while safeguarding its significant cultural and natural assets. The master plan presents the vision, planning concepts, a development framework, and standards to guide the phased implementation of Saigon South.

The community will provide the existing city and new residents with a range of needed facilities, including cultural, recreational, educational, and development opportunities. The development zone of Saigon South is framed by a parkway on the north and a scenic riverway on the south. Riverbank habitats are preserved to maintain a sustainable ecology.

Planned transportation development focuses on improving the poorly developed north-south connections to the existing city, creating new east-west connections, and designing for a pedestrian and transit-oriented transportation network. An east-west transportation system consisting of roadways and transit reserve links the development districts of Saigon South.

The new city center will consist of a series of compact walkable neighborhoods defined by an extensive system of waterways. Each district within the city center will have its own sense of identity.

182

RENDERINGS BY CHRISTOPHER GRUBBS

Santa Monica Civic Center Specific Plan
Santa Monica, California
Roma Design Group

Although Santa Monica has one of the most vibrant and enjoyable downtowns in California, the civic center is all but deserted after 5 p.m. and on weekends. Several blocks south of the bustling Third Street Promenade, a 45-acre civic center comprises an isolated cluster of public buildings, wide streets, and a sea of parking.

The Civic Center Specific Plan calls for a town square in front of city hall, a ribbon of parks connecting to nearby Palisades Park overlooking the Pacific Ocean, expanded headquarters for the nearby RAND Corporation, apartments and condominiums along Ocean Avenue, parking, and a cultural park.

The town square will serve as an interchange for citywide buses, local shuttle services, and light rail. The plan also calls for traffic calming elements such as wider sidewalks and a round-about at the south end of the site.

Santa Monica Beach Improvement
Santa Monica, California
Wallace Roberts & Todd

The Santa Monica Beach Improvement Group project is a linear park stretching nearly 3 miles along the edge of the Pacific. The park consists of a number of contiguous project areas, from the Palisades Park, a lush Victorian landscape perched high atop coastal cliffs, to South Beach, a sandy, low-lying continuation of the water's edge and home to Santa Monica's famous Muscle Beach, Chess Park, and other venues along a pedestrian promenade.

Palisades Park can be understood as a natural theater with a view to a boundless horizon, one of the great constants in nature. Yet the edge is also a palpable reminder of the fragility of nature, of how the ebbs and flows of permanence and change, the enduring and the ephemeral, have a foothold in the Palisades. The design of this park need not create drama, merely tap it.

Conversely, South Beach can be understood as a human theater. The beach boardwalk lies low in the landscape. Its edge is a mere line on the sand, and views from it are of things near—mostly of people playing, flexing, promenading, gliding on rollers or wheels, or spiking a ball high in the air. As in the Palisades, the design of the boardwalk need not create drama, merely tap it. Yet unlike the Palisades, the stage must be created. What is needed is a collection of open flexible venues for impromptu performances.

Mission Bay Master Plan

San Francisco, California
Skidmore, Owings, & Merrill

Mission Bay is a 315-acre former rail-yard site at the foot of the popular South of Market area in San Francisco, cradled by the China Basin shoreline and Potrero Hill. A new neighborhood will be an extension of the surrounding city street grid. The intersection of these streets provides direct views to parks and the waterfront. The central neighborhood is buffered from the freeway and King Street with mid-rise office and research and development buildings. The residential area will have a density and texture that will resemble a traditional San Francisco neighborhood. A dual set of retail commercial streets will provide both large- and small-scale shopping amenities for the neighborhood and San Francisco. In addition, the plan calls for public uses including a school, fire station, and community theater.

The Mission Bay neighborhood will be intersected with a system of parks containing recreation fields, contemplative spaces, and interpretive features. The parks at Mission Bay will provide significantly more open space to the residences than any other San Francisco neighborhood, creating views to parks where long distance views to the bay are not possible. The streets at Mission Bay will have a diverse role as they address different uses: Third and Fourth Streets will be retail streets. King Street will contain mid-rise office and retail space at the ground floor, and Muni Metro transit in the center median.

Crescent Park is designed to be the centerpiece of the Mission Bay neighborhood, and is part of a series of axial parks fronted by residential development with a unified architectural character. Pavilion restaurants activate Long Bridge Street and its neighborhood retail. Mission Creek divides the property into two areas. Higher density housing will create an urban edge on the north side with a view across to the south side neighborhood and houseboat area. A pedestrian bridge will connect the two areas on the Fifth Street axis.

184

RENDERINGS BY NORM KONDY

Therapeutic Garden for Children
Wellesley, Massachusetts
Douglas Reed Landscape Architecture
Child Associates,
schematic design and landform

The purpose of this project for the Institute for Child & Adolescent Development is to develop a garden that children and therapists will use for the treatment of childhood behavioral disorders resulting from trauma. The thesis of the garden is that the interaction with landscape designed for therapeutic purposes enables a child to enter the deepest reaches of self. While the garden provides opportunities for play, it primarily offers unprogrammed and evocative spaces for a child to experience. During therapy in the garden, child and therapist explore the inner world of the patient and help the child express and master basic emotions. At each session the therapist records the child's activity and behavior on a map of the garden to document the landscape's role in the therapeutic process. The garden is also used to train inner-city paraprofessionals to identify and treat traumatized children.

The 1-acre site is adjacent to the institute and contains mature oak and beech trees. A lawn swale, formerly a stream, with a 9-foot change in elevation traverses the site and is part of a series of dendritic water courses that exist in the neighborhood. This natural configuration of the site provides the inspiration for the garden's design.

The design expresses the narrative of a watercourse that weaves its way through the site, linking a sequence of spaces that correspond to stages of a child's recovery. The topography of the site has been shaped into a series of archetypal land forms carved by water: a cavelike ravine for safety and security, an upland wooded plateau for exploration, a mount for climbing, an island for seclusion, a pond for discovery, steep and shallow slopes that invite risk, and a large sunny glade for running and playing. The water course, the unifying element of the garden, originates on a terrace off the playroom of the clinic in a low granite basin. Water bubbles up, spills over the basin's edges, and travels underground in stainless steel pipes to emerge from a fieldstone sitting wall. The water then splashes into an 8-inch-wide, steel-sided rill that meanders through the garden and flows into a pond.

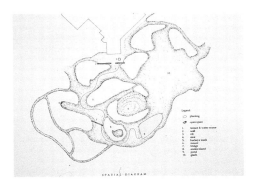

Tsukuba Institute of SANDOZ

Tsukuba, Japan
Toru Mitani,
Sasaki Environment Design Office
Fumihiko Maki, architect

This courtyard is aimed at providing refreshment and relaxation to the eye of the scientists who work in the Institute. Although the client wanted a kind of "natural" green garden, the solution to this request is a design that thoroughly inquires about the green materiality of plants. The theme is the possibility of spacemaking using the "idea" of green. In other words, how far could the plants as the living things go toward achieving a strong sense of space, not by their shape but by their texture. This garden may be an "abstract expression" of the plant's greenness.

All plants used in this garden are popular in the traditional Japanese garden: the green of azalea and the green of sasa and the green of Japanese maple. These plants are confined within meaningless geometry in order to diminish their individuality of form and enhance the reality of the texture. What people see, then, are only the subtle differences of the plant color and texture, and dramatic seasonal changes of early summer flowering and deep red leaves in the autumn. This garden could be, therefore, a quiet space fulfilled of pure green itself.

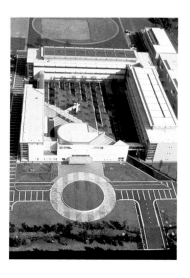

**Wind Hill Crematory
and Funeral Hall**
Nakatsu, Japan
Toru Mitani,
Sasaki Environment Design Office
Fumihiko Maki, architect

Wind Hill is a park that includes a crematorium and funeral hall to serve families from the city of Nakatsu and people who visit for funeral ceremonies. The district is very old, and many ancient ruins and tombs have been excavated. The design celebrates the earth, reflecting the archeological culture of the site. During construction, several ancient tombs were found on the site and subsequently incorporated into the park's design.

A shallow concave oval, 360 feet by 230 feet, incorporates a composition of quadratic forms. The oval is tilted slightly toward the south, as if it were one of the ancient earthworks. The higher north ridge of the oval holds the crematory building as an integrated part of the earthwork; fragments of the architectural wall emerge in sculpture. The south ridge of the oval blocks the view of the surrounding houses, providing a view toward Mt. Hachimen in the distance. A walkway around the oval is a designed as a compass to reveal a visitor's exact orientation at any point. At the center of this earthwork is a seating area called a "wind bench," where people may experience a quiet place and hear wind music created by a weather vane at the entrance gate.

Houston Police Officers Memorial
Houston, Texas
The Office of James Burnett

This memorial is dedicated to Houston police officers who gave their lives in the line of duty. It honors not only those who died, but also those brave men and women who risk their lives daily serving the citizens of Houston. The structure measures 120 feet by 120 feet and is located at the center of a 3-acre site. Its form is based on a massive stepped pyramid surrounded by four 40-foot-square amphitheaters. The memorial summit is a fountain surrounded by a polished granite ledge engraved with the names of the fallen officers.

The monument's form and materials are metaphors for the qualities of the officers it honors. The granite slabs are solid and ordered in a hierarchy of modularly sized squares. Corners and edges are crisp, clean, and square. The form reflects a ruled and rigid echelon in its symmetry and formal order. Given the importance of fraternity among officers, the memorial is not climbed in a linear fashion; its alternating steps invite a more encompassing view of the spaces. The turf within the monument is solid and clipped in contrast to a wildflower-filled meadow beyond the memorial's borders.

Burnaby Metrotown Civic Center

Burnaby, British Columbia
The SWA Group

Burnaby officials decided to create a distinctive civic center for their growing community. James K.M. Cheng Architects worked closely with The SWA Group to prepare the master plan for this three-block civic center, which would include a main library and center for the performing arts flanking a civic square, an art gallery to the west, city administration buildings (east and south of the library), and a museum. The library and most of the central civic space are built over a two-level underground parking structure. To avoid the restrictions on tree use placed on a rooftop landscape, SWA planted two rows of honey locusts in tree wells suspended in the garage.

The design provides a forced perspective focusing on the eastern civic band shell and flanking colonnades, giving a stronger sense of civic grandeur and the illusion of a more prominent civic space. The forced perspective is strengthened by a parterre of garden grids and fountains, dramatizing the site of the future performing arts center.

To avoid an architecturally impressive but little-used civic center, SWA created a variety of uses that will attract strong foot traffic. An outdoor children's garden and a native flower garden border the library. The arbor-backed band shell serves as a public amphitheater. Finally, the civic square serves as open space for an adjacent high-rise for the elderly.

The Wood and the Cemetery of the Souls

Tolosa, Spain
Iñaki Albisu Aparicio

This project was conceived as a dwelling place for the most spiritual part of the population of Tolosa: the souls, who will seek shelter in the gardens surrounding the town's old medieval church.

The north and south environments of the church are two very different zones. The north side incorporates an artificial woodland, constructed as a place of magic connotations with a dramatic invocation of nature. Big serrated rocks have been drilled to give shelter to the dry trunks of the Acadia trees, from which cables and spotlights hang like foliage. The south side of the church was formerly a palace garden. The Cemetery of Souls is represented by its paving—concrete slabs with similar dimensions to those of men, so that they may be read as tombstones on graves. The area is treated with the greatest simplicity to obtain, by means of emptiness, a sense of spirituality.

188

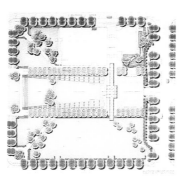

PHOTOGRAPHS BY DIXI CARRILLO

Center for Contemporary Graphic Art

Sukagawa, Japan
The SWA Group

When the Dai Nippon Printing Company, the largest in the world, acquired a large graphics collection in 1992, the company built the triangular-shaped Center for Contemporary Graphic Art outside of Sukagawa City in Fukushima Prefecture north of Tokyo. The building, designed by ED2 International Architects, is clad in white aluminum panels and includes a gallery, reception area and bookstore, audiovisual and conference rooms, and a two-story curatorial and print storage vault.

At the entrance visitors' attention is drawn to the highly geometric gallery. The entrance court is paved with two-tone gray granite that echoes the building's geometry. The triangular paving pattern evolves into a pair of highly polished black granite pyramidal fountains that flank the main doors and direct the visitor to the entry foyer. Defining the court are arches that frame landscape views to the north and south. Beyond the entrance court, visitor parking is compartmentalized by a series of clipped hedges and rows of trees. The design provides shade and reinforces the geometric nature of the building, screening the parking from the building entrance. Finally, small gardens fill spaces formed by the saw-tooth building footprint, providing outdoor space for sculptures.

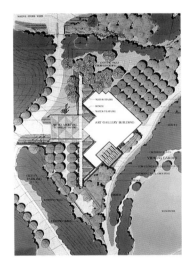

PHOTOGRAPHS BY TOM FOX

Port of Seattle Pier 69

Seattle, Washington
Murase Associates

The Port of Seattle requested a space that would be inviting to guests, clients, and employees. It was important that the port, a major Pacific Rim trading center, have a setting appropriate for hosting receptions and gatherings. The decision to renovate Pier 69 reflects the Port's commitment to preserve a working waterfront and restore a historic former cannery. A focal point of the renovation was a second floor atrium, where the landscape architect proposed a long interior water feature stretching through the building.

Upon entry to the second floor, a curved granite bench is punctuated with wedge-shaped cutouts from which water pours into a channel cut into slate pavers. The channel and bench were designed to curve against the building's rigorous structure to create an inviting and lyrical form. The channel straightens but is positioned slightly off the center axis of the powerful rectangular interior. The channel terminates at a granite tower, where the water flows gently down a curved face.

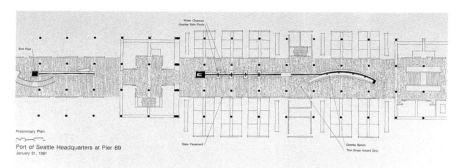

Preliminary Plan

Port of Seattle Headquarters at Pier 69
January 31, 1991

Museo de las Culturas del Norte

Paquimé, Mexico

Mario Schjetnan, José Luis Pérez
Grupo de Diseño Urbano

The Museum is located in Paquimé, in Casas Grandes, a small town in the State of Chihuahua, Mexico. Paquimé is an outstanding archeological zone in the north of Mexico, with ruins of an extensive Pueblo settlement of the 12th to the 16th centuries. The site, a flat and wide valley in the Chihuahuan Desert, is bordered to the north by a river valley forested with elms. The archeological character, the historical and monumental presence of the ruins, and the site's natural beauty create specific constraints in this delicate environment.

The concept is to create a small museum housing video and graphic material, information, a museum shop, children's discovery center, administration, curatorial and restoration shops, a cafeteria, and a central courtyard with a covered-pergola terrace. The latter is designed to accommodate theater, folk dances, and crafts sessions.

The exhibit rooms will showcase the rich archeological and ethnographic material that has been collected, and the exhibits will be enhanced with models and interactive videos. Each showroom is related to an open court-yard and designed to portray a specific natural theme: the first is circular with the theme of the desert. The second, a long rectangular room, directs views toward the mountains, with the theme of dry river beds. The third, a triangular courtyard, is based on the pine forests of the sierras.

The museum building is excavated into the existing terrain, creating a system of berms, varied forms, and inclines covered with desert vegetation. These forms enclose a roof terrace and integrate the museum with its natural landscape.

Rancho la Puerta Spa

Tecate, Mexico
Chris Drayer Landscape Architect

Over a ten year period, an upgrade of the facilities and a complete redesign of more than 30 acres of grounds was completed at a well-known, 56-year-old health resort just across the United States-Mexico border from San Diego, California. The goal of the project was to create a memorable space imbued with both the unique character of the surrounding chaparral landscape and the traditional imagery of an oasis while retaining the resort's historical connections.

In addition to designing the gardens and landscape, the landscape architect was also responsible for remodeling the existing buildings and designing many of the new ones, with the idea of achieving a seamless blending of buildings and landscape. The project was also seen as an opportunity to demonstrate ecologically sensitive design, construction, and maintenance practices. Wastewater is recycled through a biological marsh system for landscape irrigation, xeriscape principles are applied to landscape design, indigenous materials and techniques are employed in construction, construction and demolition debris are recycled, and native species have been restored on degraded land.

Cheney Cowles Museum
Spokane, Washington
Jim Kavelage
BOORA Architects

The proposed Cheney Cowles Museum is a 122,000-square-foot complex designed to preserve and interpret regional and American histories and the visual arts. Its site at 2316 First Avenue nestles into Browne's Addition, one of the oldest, most beautiful neighborhoods in the region, and is in close proximity to the historical encampment site of the Plateau Indians. Perched on a bluff overlooking the valley of the Spokane River, the museum is configured to embrace a sunken courtyard defined by both building walls and the topography of the hillside. The courtyard accommodates outdoor exhibition and performance spaces, allows natural light to enter the lower levels, and frames views of the valley for both interior and exterior spaces. Inscribed in the courtyard is a large circular area of compacted earth for Native American storytelling and cultural events. Columnar basalt will be used to create a waterfall of both cascade and plunge-pool form.

A variety of environments are created in the galleries through a series of terraced platforms constructed of rammed earth. Wide ramps descend to the two-story volume of the underground galleries, where skylights—conceived as sculptural objects or rock outcroppings in the garden—and large north-facing windows provide natural light. The north gallery merges with the natural landscape of the hillside, its rooftop a meadow of native grasses where a canoe-shaped skylight washes the stone gallery wall below.

Hautana Housing Area
Boeblingen, Germany
Bernd Krüger, Hubert Möhrle

The housing block is characterized by a symmetric assembly of point houses with connecting flat buildings. This housing arrangement achieves superior daylight qualities for the apartments and good ventilation of the complex. The living quality of the housing is improved by the possibility of parties, games, and relaxation areas in the courtyard.

A U-shaped form around resident gardens, a small lake, and trees defines the courtyard space. The courtyard is separated from public access by a high-rise wooden deck with a grid of sweet chestnut trees. The resulting level difference is accentuated optically and acoustically with a waterfall. Each ground-level flat has a planted terrace with a private garden. The materials for path edges and planters coincide with the construction materials of the building—wood, concrete, and metal.

The complex is surrounded with angled parking spaces and pedestrian walkways covered with trees. The adjacent office block is connected by a pedestrian area with trees over the underground garage.

Rainwater from the roofs is fed into the beds of the courtyard. The rest of the water is fed into an overflow tank to supply the lake with water. The waterfall is fed with lake water which is then resupplied to the lake.

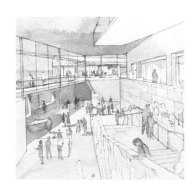

Koga City Folk Museum Garden

Koga City, Japan
Shodo Suzuki
Landscape Architect and Associates

Koga City is a historic city in Ibaraki Prefecture. This project is an integration of the preservation of a castle and a park around a museum in which the city maintains treasures from Senseki Takami, a famous scholar of Dutch studies in the Edo Period. The site also includes Takami's house.

The design intent was not only to preserve a historic site, but to revive it and craft a new environment for visitors by creating a new waterfront along a canal that flows through the property. The project is divided into three areas: the garden in front of the museum, the area around the scholar's historic house, and roads around the site.

A garden in front of the museum incorporates a pond, from where water flows into a waterfall into the canal. Black polished granite and white pebbles evoke the image of the black and white world of traditional Japanese calligraphy. The banks of the canal, once fabricated of compacted soil, are now made of stones with a modern finish. The water is shallow so that children can play in the water, and a fountain expresses the forms of reeds in the wind. Lines of cobblestones at the bottom of the pond can be seen through the water. A pavilion and bicycle parking are located near this feature. Roads around the site are paved with cobblestones that match the finishes of the canal, stone walls, pathways, and other landscape materials.

Takami's house was renovated and is now used as a tea house with a tea garden in which old trees and unusual species are maintained.

Palm Drive Reconstruction Project

Stanford University, California
Stanford University Planning Office,
Judy Chan, landscape architect
Tom Richman and Associates,
landscape architecture consultants
Brian Kongas Foulk, engineers

This project focused on reconstructing the signature entry to Stanford University, where traffic safety concerns needed to be addressed as well as drainage problems, deteriorated road conditions, regional traffic needs, and long-term maintenance costs. Additionally, the project team was required to maintain the historic integrity of the entry, restore elements of the original Frederick Law Olmsted campus plan, and protect and preserve historic palm trees. The approach taken by the project team was to develop solutions based on "how it works" and "how it feels." In this way a variety of complex factors including historical context, esthetics, engineering worthiness, and functional needs were balanced.

Archival research uncovered Olmsted's original, never built, granite curb design. This historical precedent was worked into a unique detail combining split-faced granite curbs and slotted edge drains, which solved the persistent drainage problem and provided edge definition. Other features include new bike lanes and pedestrian paths, and runoff drains that lead to seasonal ponds in an adjacent arboretum, recharging ground water and enhancing wildlife habitat. One hundred fifty-two historic palm trees were evaluated and treated individually by a palm specialist. Additional native species were selected for roadway planting beneath the palms. The university's signature vista was preserved by prohibiting left turns at a major intersection and avoiding the use of traffic signal mast arms.

As a focal element of the campus plan, Palm Drive is one of the most sacred outdoor spaces in the western United States, creating a mile-long vista to the university's Memorial Church. By using Olmsted's vision as a foundation, the project team struck an optimal balance between esthetics, history, and modern functional needs, providing adequate road capacity while preserving the historic roadway's character.

Secondary School

Ticino, Switzerland
Paolo L. Bürgi

The theme of this project is the recovery of the waters, a topical subject where ecology is interpreted in an actual language, in dialogue with our landscape. Artifice stays recognizable.

Rainwater collected on roofs and plazas returns to subterranean strata, leaving traces in its path. On the soil it generates a particular vegetation, whereas on the plaza it makes stains on the fountain's concrete, thanks to the temporal detention of water which gradually drains and, in excess, overflows into a raised iron grid.

Access from the road to this plaza is provided through wide concrete ramp-stairs with a handmade relief on the surface. Across the plaza, on the opposite side, is access to the sport fields; here the stairs grow grass on the treads.

At the inner part of the school is a secluded, quiet courtyard, inspired by the surrounding countryside. A long curved bench invites people to rest in the sun or shade.

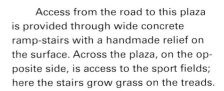

The Neurosciences Institute

La Jolla, California
Burton Associates, landscape architects;
Tod Williams Billie Tsien & Associates,
architects

The Neurosciences Institute is an independent research organization dedicated to understanding the functions of the brain. In 1991, the institute relocated from the campus of Rockefeller University in New York to the Scripps Campus in La Jolla, California, to take advantage of opportunities for expansion and to tap into the scientific research resources of the region whose residents include the Salk Institute and La Jolla Cancer Research Institute. The architecture firm of Tod Williams Billie Tsien & Associates designed the campus as a "monastery for science." Three structures compose the "cloister": a three-story theory center and a bermed laboratory wing form a U-shaped ensemble of buildings oriented to the east. An acoustically superior auditorium with a bermed mechanical wing humanizes the scale of the winding plaza. Burton Associates' job was to develop a dialogue between the buildings and the site, and to design all exterior project spaces.

Like the process of discovery, the Neurosciences Institute reveals itself gradually. In fact, it is impossible to take in all of the complex at once, and views shift dramatically depending on one's vantage point. The upper tier of the project is composed of plantings of native or naturalized species which will, when mature, provide a backdrop. The landscape of the plaza embraces few elements: a single linear planting of timber bamboo on the lower plaza level, a reflective pool, and a stand of horsetail at the metaphorical river one crosses to enter the theory center. A lone Torrey pine at the auditorium forecourt allows this unique tree to be viewed as a specimen, in contrast to those that grow naturally on the hillsides of this region. A grass berm is planted with a small copse of California pepper, referring to the distant view of the surrounding hills and providing movement from the ocean breezes. Niche planting of *Melaleuca nesophylla* offers a whimsical note along the upper walkway, which connects the institute to the Scripps campus through a tunnel under a road.

196

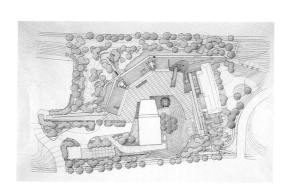

Library Walk

San Diego, California
Peter Walker William Johnson
and Partners

The campus of the University of California at San Diego evolved over several decades on a series of high bluffs in Southern California. The original site included a very large plantation of eucalyptus, which had proved uneconomical for harvesting as building timber. Left to grow to maturity, these eucalyptus groves had developed into forests that have been used as settings for individual university buildings and works of art and are among the most beautiful areas of the campus today.

In most other areas of the campus, however, piecemeal development and lack of strong spatial structure in the overall planning had produced an impression of disorder and confusion. Thus, when Peter Walker William Johnson and Partners were brought in to work on a new campus mall, they began to study not only the mall's site, but also the patterns of circulation and spatial structure of the campus as a whole.

The program called for the creation of a major linear space that would join a newly enlarged library, student center, and a series of university-wide classroom buildings and counseling rooms, along with the university's newly expanded medical school. The landscape architects proposed that such a space should be integrated with an existing pedestrian path that runs along the major axis of the campus, leading ultimately up to the library, the campus's symbolic center.

The landscape architects proposed to relate the modules and scale of the path to the modules and scale of the various buildings along the way. Near many of the classrooms the scale would be made more intimate, and near the medical school, an architecturally more ambitious complex, the scale would be larger and more monumental. This bold composition of paving patterns, seat walls, platforms for public speaking, small adjacent spaces for meeting and resting, and reinforced views into the nearby eucalyptus groves helps link the many points along the axial path, bringing together natural and formal elements into one strong statement of the open space and pedestrian organization of the campus.

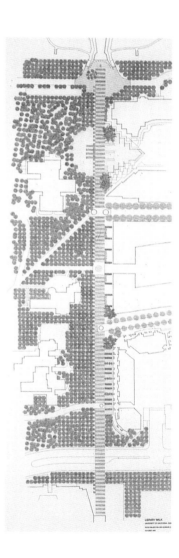

Center for Advanced Science and Technology

Harima Science Garden City, Japan
Peter Walker William Johnson
and Partners

The Center for Advanced Science and Technology (CAST) is an international meeting place for the exchange of ideas among scientists, Nobel laureates, and political leaders. With a major building by Arata Isozaki, it is also an important cultural landmark.

Approaching the center through a natural forest, one arrives at the campus garden, a stylized archipelago of regular mounds that recall small mountains. On the summit of each mound is a cypress tree with a red light at the top; the mounds represent the volcanic activity that originally formed the mountains in the immediate environment. Walking past these mounds, one enters the CAST complex.

From the glass walls of the director's offices and through the windows of another wing of the building, one can view another garden, a plane of lawn and gravel paths, shaded by an informal pine grove. Extending across the lawn and paths is a grid of still, round pools lying flush with the ground plane. By day, these pools reflect the sky, the building, and the people who walk in the garden. At night, the pools glow from within, illuminating the underside of the pines.

A third garden, adjacent to the hotel and conference area, is designed mainly for contemplation. Rising from a "sea" of raked gravel are a "mountain" of stone and a "mountain" of moss. Running between the two mountains is a straight line of large stepping stones that lead into the building. This path is intersected by a straight line of ancient wooden logs, which also extend through the building. Framing these elements is a regular grove of bamboo—from which mist rises at intervals, pulsating and flooding the garden with dense moisture so that only the tips of the mountains remain visible for a time.

198

Kempinski Hotel

Munich, Germany
Peter Walker William Johnson
and Partners

The landscape design for the Kempinski Hotel and the Munich Airport Center were conceived as a series of interacting spaces that achieve the client's mandate of "an airport in the countryside." An overall structure of allées, groves, and plantings along the streets, paths, and in parking lots is combined with a sequence of special places—parks, gardens, glazed plazas—that offer variety and a memorable sense of place.

The sequence of places are experienced as four distinct gardens. First is a series of linear gardens that accompany the moving sidewalk. Here, formal rows and beds form a series of continuous green passages of low hedges alternating with pyramidal evergreens and poplars. Groves of white birch, rising from beds of colored gravels and spring bulbs, distinguish the intersections. As one approaches the hotel, a garden of stone, gravel, and hedges recalls the region's agricultural landscape.

The second garden is the arrival garden for the Kempinski Hotel. On the ground are stone and concrete pavers overlaid by a series of interlocking stone rings, a series of interrupted hedges, and rows of European hornbeam. An informal grove of pine directs visitors into either of the building entries.

Third is the great hotel atrium, a partly covered space divided diagonally into a formal lobby and sitting garden, and a dining and festivities terrace. The atrium garden is made of ivy topiary hedges, garden-like paving, and small pools of light. Furniture carries out the garden theme. The terrace includes a bar in a grove of palm trees; on the terrace, steel trellis "trees" are planted inside and out with flowering vines. Separating the two sides of the atrium are dividing panels of window boxes made of transparent glass planted with geraniums.

The fourth garden, a formal parterre, is the centerpiece. Conceived as a place for strolling, sitting, and relaxation, much as a public park might be, this garden is a weaving of two grids, articulated in low border hedges, colored gravel, columnar oaks, lawn, and boxed hedges.

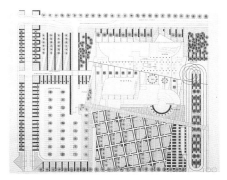

Courtyard for the German Institute of Standards
Berlin, Germany
Richard Weller; in collaboration with Muller, Knippschild, Wehberg

The German Institute of Standards (the Deutsche Institute Normen, or DIN) has its central office in Berlin. To cope with the enormous increase in work and status as Berlin expanded from Cold War enclave to a boom town metropolis, a dark, sober, rectilinear bureaucratic building was converted into a dark, reflective, and slightly angular bureaucratic building.

The workers in the building all had various pictures of artwork, relatives, or holiday resorts pinned to the walls of their offices. Our task was to provide them with what is in essence another picture—that of a courtyard garden viewed only by those who work within. No one actually has access to the garden, which is constructed on 60 centimeters of earth above a two-story parking garage.

An institute of standards conducts the meticulous work of standardizing everything and, in Germany at least, this can reach tyrannical extremes. This project is thus intended as a postmodern quip: A piece of A4 paper, which is a standard DIN product and also the paper that the workers in the building write on, has "fallen" out of the window and landed awkwardly in the courtyard. The A4 paper, in the form of a 16-by-7-meter granite slab, is engraved with the DIN letterhead in stainless steel; water flows over the slab, where stainless steel letters form a text. Bosquets and lines of trees surround the whole space, and when other buildings around the courtyard invest in landscape, as their owners have agreed to, the plan can be simply extended. Thus, the landscape is a standardized commodity, an extendible logo that each development can fill in at any time.

Green Pia Tsunan Central Garden
Tsunan-cho, Japan
Yoshiki Toda

Green Pia Tsunan is a health resort for pensioners. Visitors may stay in the resort and enjoy the surrounding recreational facilities, which include ski slopes, a camping area, tennis courts, and an indoor swimming pool.

A central garden adjacent to the hotel was inspired by a local mountain stream whose seven waterfalls are known as "Nanatsu-gama" (Seven Pots). Surrounded by mountains, this area sees a heavy snowfall, and the natural water supply flowing from the mountains was incorporated into the garden plan, which integrates a stream, ponds, seven waterfalls, and large lawns.

A stone artwork placed in the upper stream represents a magical icework called "Kami-watari" (God's Passing) that is seen when a nearby lake freezes. A round pond in the lower stream mirrors the sky and reflects the changing of the seasons.

200

Osaka City University Media Center Plaza

Osaka, Japan
Makoto Naborisaka, David Buck
Nikken Sekkei

Osaka City University is situated in a quiet residential neighborhood in the southern part of the city. The University Media Center, a 10-story aluminum-clad building and its surrounding plaza represent the first implemented phase of a new campus-wide master plan. The traditional pattern of universities in Japan as enclosed, hallowed grounds of learning gave way here to an open plaza, which grew out of discussions with the local residents. The plaza was in one sense a memorial gift from the university to the citizens. What would be our gift as designers to the students and residents, and how could we form a relationship between them, the media center, and the landscape?

It seemed logical to use words, taken from the pages of library texts and scatter them around the site like found objects, snapshots of our knowledge of the natural world. We chose landscape emotions and landscape ecology as the main themes for a series of cast aluminum nameplates to introduce nature in the urban environment and to establish a link between man, the natural environment, and natural processes. Arranged on a grid within the paving, grouped around benches, and dotted around the pool and planting, the nameplate words are for the citizens and students to read, study, or survey, a metaphorical and physical link that questions our ideas of nature and what it means in the modern city. There is a certain ironic undertone in our decision to use man-made cast aluminum to evoke nature and an emotional interaction with the landscape.

The main plaza is 70 by 40 meters in area, located immediately in front of the building, and facing the adjacent residential area. The central focus of the site is a 20-by-30-meter pool, 17 centimeters deep, bisected by a cast aluminum bridge. Four meters wide and based on a 50-centimeter-square module, the bridge extends beyond the edge of the pool, linking the site symbolically to the surrounding residential area. Wooden benches under double rows of crape myrtle and evergreen dogwood offer shaded refuge.

The first group of 52 words are evocative of human interaction with the natural landscape: *awe, mystery, fear, illusion*. These words attempt to draw out memories from earlier, more primitive times as well as elicit a response from the present designed setting. Next are 39 plates that introduce some of the key concepts from the field of landscape ecology: *mosaic sequence, species flow, ecological integrity*. The last group of 28 has the names of key figures who have contributed to this field, from Harvard Professor Richard Forman to German ecologist Karl-Friedrich Schreiber. No list can ever be fully representative or comprehensive, so blank nameplates are included for future discoveries in landscape ecology or to fill in the gaps in individual experiences. For a book-return element, we proposed an enlarged replica of Darwin's *Origin of Species* as a symbol commemorating Darwin's role as the world's first ecologist. Cast in aluminum, the representation includes the complete contents, cover symbol, title, and texture of the original. Standing in front of the main entrance, this enlarged "volume" clarifies the building's function and marks Darwin's contribution to the field of ecology.

Oyama Training Center

Oyama, Japan
Peter Walker William Johnson
and Partners

The Tokyo Marine Training Center is set among traditional farms in the countryside north of Tokyo in an emerging housing, office, and retail development. The setting responds to a range of new functions while reflecting a memory of the gradually disappearing agricultural landscape. Rather than evoke nostalgia for the past, however, the new setting invites quiet contemplation among elements of the traditional agricultural landscape that have been borrowed and ultimately transformed.

The landscape architects viewed this training center, with its offices, classrooms, and accommodations for dining and congregating, as an agricultural villa and garden. A triple allée of poplars surrounds the site, allowing one to walk in the shade and glimpse both the villa-garden complex and the landscape beyond. Across the rolling ground plane are bands of field grasses and gravel paths, arranged in geometric patterns. From ground level, and particularly from the offices above, these radiating patterns are designed to recall the patterns of cultivated fields.

Elsewhere in the complex, courtyards feature more familiar elements of the garden and the farm. In one graveled courtyard, a wall, half-circular in plan, rises to a lattice planted in wisteria. A large circular planter of bamboo with delicate, pale leaves catches the light from above.

In the "castle" garden is a series of hedges pruned to form "crenellations" recalling castle walls. Running between these hedges is a secret pool, half hidden from the open circular lawn and fountain. This large garden was designed for informal gatherings, parties, and ceremonies.

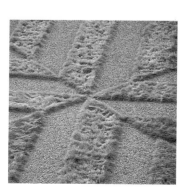

YKK Research and Development Center

Tokyo, Japan
Toru Mitani,
Sasaki Environment Design Office
Fumihiko Maki, architect

This 6,900-square-foot office courtyard is located on a third-floor rooftop, surrounded by a research and design center, a large presentation hall, and many office floors. As office workers look down into this space throughout the year, the garden has been designed as a reflection of changes that occur in the natural surroundings and changes in humans' outdoor activities.

The simple geometry of the garden reflects change. A circle of black granite, moistened by a mist fountain, produces a mirrored surface reflecting the color changes of the sky during the day. A grove of bamboo waves in the air stream generated between the buildings. In front of the president's room are 55 "wind-fish" (a kind of weather vane). These red fish are small and visually strong only when they all move together in a sudden gust of wind.

Great West Life Corporate Garden
Denver, Colorado
Civitas

Great West Life challenged the design team, a collaboration between artist/sculptor Larry Kirkland and the landscape architectur firm, Civitas, to create an evocative new garden for its U.S. headquarters. With the freedom to pursue a range of design ideas, the team decided to create a space that would take employees away from their everyday office experience and immerse them in a stimulating landscape.

The garden is anchored by a large shade pergola intended to represent shelter. Below the structure is a sunken room which provides steps as seats and allows users to enjoy two granite fountains that oscillate in flow from a frothing cone to a rushing wedge. Nine sculptures add domestic symbols, from a 6-foot vase of flowers on a table to a 13-foot abstract figure. The garden is surrounded by native trees, shrubs, flowers, and ornamental grasses.

Ocean Spray Cranberries Headquarters
Middleboro, Massachusetts
Carol R. Johnson Associates

The site, with a highly scenic, rural New England agricultural character, was established as a corporate headquarters for Ocean Spray Cranberries. The cranberry bogs remain in active production and are a dominant visual reinforcement of the origins of Ocean Spray. The design involved constructing corporate headquarters, replicating wetlands, revitalizing aquatic habitat, and restoring built areas to indigenous landscape.

The cranberry crop is the most valuable per acre crop in American agriculture. The bogs, which depend on the availability of water for irrigation, frost protection, and harvesting, had been supported by a 35-acre pond. The pond had been created some 20 years earlier by damming a brook and flooding a broad lowland area. Due to underlying organic soils and shallow depth, eutrophication was consuming the pond. During the summer months, heavy weed growth and algae choked the entire pond. Except for stretches a few feet wide along the former brook channel, weed growth consumed the entire volume of the pond from the bottom to within inches of the surface.

Nearly half the existing pond was dredged to provide habitat variation and enhance the character. The hydraulic dredging of the pond produced more than 100,000 cubic yards of exceptional loam when blended with the sand of the embankments of the sedimentation pools.

The pond, with a variety of habitats, provides an exceptional natural foreground for the arrival to the site. Upon entering the site, one sees the distant view of the headquarters building across the pond. The arrival sequence continues as the roadway skirts the pond, winds through the woodland, crosses the bogs, and terminates at a court at the building entry.

American College Testing Corporate Campus
Des Moines, Iowa
Herbert Lewis Kruse Blunck
Architecture

Herbert Lewis Kruse Blunck Architecture designed the master plan to unify the existing American College Testing corporate campus, including 450,000 square feet of future buildings. The goals were identified as providing for phased building expansion, incorporating the natural site amenities, utilizing existing roads and parking, allowing for a sense of completeness at each stage of development, providing infrastructure to accommodate future growth, and minimizing the visual impact of parking.

The design solution incorporated the following features: existing parking lots were expanded with minimal disruption; parking lots were located on the periphery and screened; existing roads were modified only as necessary; a new ring road was created to establish a campus green; natural landscape was continued from the woodlands and existing plants and ravines; a central plaza was created as a focal point; and a processional alleé of coniferous trees was created to connect the plaza and a new amphitheater.

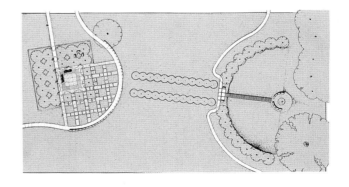

Hewlett Packard Roseville Campus

Roseville, California
The SWA Group

Hewlett Packard's service, repair, and distribution complex on 500 acres of rolling grassland no longer served the company's needs and would not support future expansion. The property's vegetation had suffered from difficult soils and long hot summers during the last eight years. Hewlett Packard wanted a new master plan that would redevelop its facility and overcome what it considered a hostile environment.

One of the most important tasks for the landscape architect was to reframe Hewlett Packard's perception of the surrounding landscape as hostile. For the vast majority of the site, we sought not to convert the grassland, but to reestablish it wherever possible by planting large fields of native grass with a rich oak woodland mix in the non-use areas. The company came to appreciate the property's unspoiled beauty.

Against the vast open plain of the Sacramento Valley grasslands, and to complement the equally vast low-profile facility, The SWA Group decided that the landscape elements needed to be extremely bold and simple to be easily understood and enjoyed. Interior and exterior spaces were connected; for example, a poplar-lined pedestrian walkway is raised above the Chinese elm-shaded parking lot and leads into the building. Bradford pear trees unify the recreational complex, which includes a baseball diamond, basketball court, and sand volleyball court. The trees also afford these large areas both scale and shade, which was considered the key to creating an attractive outdoor landscape that Hewlett Packard's employees would actually use and enjoy. We focused on introducing plants that would both provide luxuriant shade and thrive despite the harsh soil and weather. To that end, we stripped the trees of root competition, freeing them from shrubs, ground covers, and lawns. We maintained a permeable ground plan by providing localized and individual watering, as well as a sub-drain system to remove any excess water caused by inherent soil permeability problems.

Courtyards were placed throughout the facility and planted primarily with Bradford pear trees to lure employees into the shaded outdoors. We also planted a lot of hardy London plane trees throughout the project to provide major shady areas.

206

Federal Reserve Bank
Dallas, Texas
The SWA Group

When the Federal Reserve's Board of Governors in Washington, D.C., decided to build the first new Federal Reserve Bank in 71 years, bank officials spent nearly a decade exhaustively researching, analyzing, and planning how to build this Dallas facility for the 21st century. The new bank had to serve all of the business needs of a central bank. It had to incorporate the newest technology in its bank management operations, mechanical systems, and security. It had to serve the general public and meet the needs of its workers. Finally, its design had to reflect the strength, dignity, and stability of a federal reserve bank while reflecting the Texan environment, history, and character.

Two firms—Sikes Jennings Kelly & Brewer of Houston and Kohn Pederson Fox of New York—were commissioned to design the complex. Completed in 1993, the Federal Reserve Bank occupies a city block at the edge of the central business district. It comprises three towers grouped around a central courtyard.

The SWA Group created a strong regional connection by using native drought-tolerant Texas plants. We began by lining the sidewalks around the bank with southern red oaks and blanketing the large pedestrian entrance with Texas red yucca planted as ground cover. The outdoor visitor parking area is spanned by cables that support wisteria vines which provide shade, shadow, and seasonal color.

The Federal Reserve Bank has two rooftop gardens that serve as breakout areas for the staff. SWA faced several conflicting requirements in their design, including weight, waterproofing, exposure, security, budget, and visual integration of the gardens with the powerful geometry of the encircling towers.

A 2-acre garden grows above the check collection department at the north end of the building. Its comblike straight walks reflect the building grid, creating long wedges of perfectly horizontal, finely textured Bermuda grass lawns, framed with taller, mature hybrid buffalo grass. A forest of river birch creates a shady separation for the lawn areas and captures the seasonal play of the architectural shadow line across the roof deck. A sinuous lateral walk holds a display garden of annuals and perennials. The bank's conference rooms, exercise facility, and day-care center open onto this garden.

The smaller courtyard garden expresses the rotation of the enclosing office towers against the rigid bank structure below with three declining wedges of green grass, surmounted with a grouping of Burr oaks that anchor the center of the garden, and a colorful ribbon of native annuals and perennials. Tall buffalo grass along the sides of the tilted wedges contrasts with the planes of clipped Bermuda grass in the lawns. The ribbon of perennials ties the three large wedges to the ground and recalls the color planting in the large garden. Offices, conference rooms, and other facilities look out onto this courtyard garden.

207

PHOTOGRAPHS BY TOM FOX

The Gardens and Shops at the Arizona Center

Phoenix, Arizona
ELS Associates, architects
The SWA Group, landscape architects

Phoenix, Arizona, has been one of the nation's fastest-growing cities since the 1970s, but it has suffered from a nondescript downtown without soul or excitement. In the 1990s city officials launched an aggressive redevelopment plan that included a number of publicly and privately funded projects, such as a new central library. The heart of that plan is the Arizona Center, an 8-square-block mixed-use site developed by the Rouse Company to act as a magnet that would attract residents and visitors back to downtown. The SWA Group created a 3-acre oasis at the heart of the Arizona Center, unifying the large site and focusing the surrounding office buildings, retail, and restaurants on a tranquil climate-mitigating desert garden.

To shelter visitors from the grueling desert sun, the Gardens employ a series of shade canopies and vine-covered ramadas. Ficus trees, mesquites, and jacarandas provide understory shade along the walkways. More than 900 mature date palms create structure and overstory shade. In a desert town whose temperature often soars to 115 degrees Fahrenheit in the summer, SWA made extensive use of water, incorporating fountains, mist, grottoes, and ponds to provide "outdoor air conditioning" that lowers the surrounding air temperature by 20 to 30 degrees and adds to the prevailing sense of tranquility and pleasure. Tiered gardens, intimate parterre gardens, a children's maze garden, dining terraces, and the promenade are all planted with native and desert plants and flowers. Viewed from overhead—many of the surrounding buildings look down on the Gardens—the landscape is designed to look like a series of waves leading to a central pool.

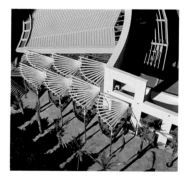

MacArthur Court

Newport Beach, California
The SWA Group

The Irvine Company owned three low-rise buildings diagonally across from the John Wayne Airport and wanted to develop the property, maintain separate identities for each building, and integrate the buildings into a cohesive whole. Skidmore, Owings, & Merrill designed two new 15-story office towers and a 4-story parking garage. The SWA Group provided site planning and planting design services for this project, which was completed in 1987. Our primary goal was to unite the disparate buildings, reflect the formal architecture, and provide a place of urbanity, elegance, and quiet beauty for the buildings' visitors and tenants.

A formal auto arrival court provides access to the new office towers. The court features a central fountain ringed by Canary Island date palms. Water from the fountain is flush with the top of the bermed turf border.

Tree hedges delineate the site's border. Plantings of date palms provide order and emphasize certain functions and buildings. Rows and bosques of date and Mexican fan palms accent and give a monumental scale. They also identify the entry areas. Rows of fan palms silhouetted against the skyline highlight the entry drive. A grid of date palms creates an interior palm court that ties together all four buildings while providing an attractive shade canopy for workers and visitors. This design creates an abstract formal landscape base that highlights the new twin office towers.

209

Solana

Westlake and Southlake, Texas
Peter Walker William Johnson
and Partners

Since 1984, the team of clients and designers planning Solana, a regional headquarters for IBM in West Texas, sought a balance of social, economic, esthetic, cultural, and environmental purposes and ideals. The complex, on an 850-acre parcel of former ranch land 20 minutes' drive from the Dallas/Ft. Worth Airport, has been designed and planned by architects Barton Myers, Mitchell/Giurgola, and Ricardo Legorreta, and landscape architects Peter Walker William Johnson and Partners. Solana, which means a "place in the sun," includes a recreation center, marketing center, and office complex, designed to house as many as 20,000 employees.

To preserve this continuous landscape of courtyards, gardens, stream bank, and prairie, the design team decided to subordinate certain features of the built landscape so that the expansive rural, once pastoral setting might be more clearly expressive of the region and its historic agricultural uses. To enhance the horizontal line of the prairie, building heights were limited to five stories and building sites were often located on relatively low ground. To keep several hundred acres open, undeveloped, and restored where necessary, buildings were clustered in traditional southwestern hacienda style.

An understanding of what should be saved informed the designer's sense of what might be changed. As the built landscape of Solana has matured, and as spaces of varying qualities and moods have taken shape, a feeling of

serenity and understatement has predominated. At Solana, buildings don't compete with one another for attention, and mundane utilitarian features such as exit ramps and parking garages are designed to shape gardens and courtyards that harmonize with the familiar rural landscape. Today, after a decade of expansion and growth, the buildings and the maturing gardens, with their blend of vernacular and distinctly modern qualities of space, form, and materials, have come to be at home in their region of West Central Texas.

Plaza Tower

Costa Mesa, California
Peter Walker William Johnson
and Partners

The Plaza Tower office development is the most recent component of South Coast Plaza Town Center, an emerging urban center in Orange County, California. This county, formerly rural and agricultural, was the site of vast suburban development in the decades immediately after World War II. Landscape architect Peter Walker began working on this site in the early 1970s, designing a 5-acre park of curves, mounds, and groves of trees. Now, with the evolution of South Coast Plaza Town Center, the complex includes a Performing Arts Center, Repertory Theater, office buildings, hotel, and a series of plazas and

spaces, including Isamu Noguchi's California Scenario. Plaza Tower, designed by architect Arata Isozaki, serves as regional headquarters for IBM and home to other corporations, professional tenants, and restaurants.

The entrance to bold, bow-fronted, stainless-steel-clad Plaza Tower is equally bold, with its geometries delineated in stainless steel and water. A series of 4-inch bands of stainless steel pulled tight across the surface of the entry court connect the tower graphically with an adjacent parking structure. Concentric stainless steel rings form a series of alternating weirs and pools to make identical fountains on either side of the entrance. Light bollards of stainless steel mark the edge of the court, providing a vertical counterpoint to the horizontal patterning.

This apparently seamless blending of structure and site is enlivened by "Utsurohi," a site-specific sculpture by Aiko Miyawaki. The sculpture comprises 12 columns representing the signs of the Japanese zodiac, connected at the top by stainless steel rods to create a kinetic tracery against the sky. Other elements of the plaza call attention to light, wind, and sky: the dense groves of poplar and purple-leaf plum near the base of the tower, the stainless steel elements that reflect the changing color and intensity of natural light, and the reflective still pools of water.

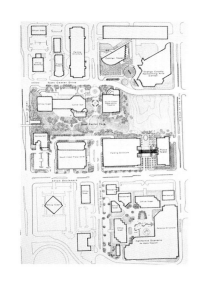

The landscape design professions have their work cut out for them. They need to enlarge public recognition of the importance of the created landscape to our cultural well-being, while simultaneously deepening the discussion among people concerned with its artistic form and social function. This entails recognizing two distinct audiences—one lay and one professional—and learning how to communicate with both of them. It is a job for designers as much as for critics and historians; we need to narrow the gulf between academics and practitioners. We need a stronger commitment to discourse within the professions and a larger arena for public address if landscape designers are ever to have a serious impact on the cultural space we inhabit.

Perhaps the emergence of the Designed Landscape Forum is a sign that these objectives can be addressed. To learn to speak, we must first learn to see. We must recognize the theoretical perspectives—both conscious and unacknowledged—that we bring to bear on the landscape. At the same time, we need to encourage the development of landscape criticism as a way of analyzing and interpreting what we build.

Theory and criticism are not distinct from practice; they are its necessary adjuncts. Theory helps us predict how a design will function in a particular set of natural and social circumstances; it also illumines the relationship between cultural transformations and changes in the land. Criticism comes after the fact. I liken it to an autopsy, not in the sense of cutting something open to see why it died, but closer to the Greek root of the word, *autopsfa*, which we might translate as "to see for oneself" or even "the act of seeing with one's own eyes." Criticism begins with description. Since we don't all see the same way, criticism enables us to recognize our individual habits of seeing and to agree generally on what it is we are observing. Then, criticism can help us analyze what we are seeing in relation to other things—to history, to the social and cultural context, and to the topographical and biological surroundings.

Such seeing is essential to the health of any kind of art and a crucial prelude to evaluating its achievements. I am basically sympathetic to the notion that a work of art isn't completed until it begins its life in public, where it is read, analyzed, and evaluated.

Yet criticism, though part of the academic experience, is scant in landscape design practice. It should be part of everyone's work: something designers apply to their own projects and to those of their peers, and something that designers, critics, and historians provide to the public. Criticism is relatively more vigorous in the other visual arts: painting, sculpture, and, architecture. Perhaps as more sculptors become engaged in landscape projects, they will bring with them the critical habits—not to mention the writers— that are more pervasive in their field. At the same time, such merging of professional interests might increase cross-disciplinary knowledge. While there are exceptions, architects, landscape architects, and sculptors remain too unfamiliar with the artistic standards and patterns of practice among their peers in other disciplines.

The landscape design professions must resolve a number of parochial matters before they can find their bearings in the world. Perhaps the Forum can help with this as well. First, a wider range of people need to be recognized for their contribution to the designed landscape—not just landscape architects, but artists, photographers, writers, and historians. This book goes beyond the limits of the typical professional journal in presenting a cross-disciplinary survey of projects by landscape architects and sculptors, but the Forum's reach could be extended still further. While enlarging the scope of the professions, the Forum might also help widen the concept of the designed landscape itself.

Most of the work presented here has distinct formal features, whether abstract or naturalistic. But less purposeful landscapes ought to be examined, including those that might be termed popular or vernacular. Likewise, there are designed landscapes without obvious formal characteristics, such as land planning and conservation projects, that are not much in evidence here. Yet the identification and preservation of significant open space strikes me as an exercise with undeniable implications for the visible form of the environment. Indeed, in an era when human intervention has changed every aspect of nature, from the dispersal and extinction of species to topography and even climate, there is simply no place apart from culture.

This publication is focused on built projects, which is fair enough in an effort to assess the state of the landscape arts. Many will be familiar to readers of the design magazines. Burton Associates' landscape for the Neurosciences Institute in La Jolla; Rios Associates' gardens for a private house in Los Angeles; and Martha Schwartz, Ken Smith, and David Meyer's sequence of public spaces for the Village of Yorkville Park in Toronto have all been published previously. But the sheer number of landscapes presented here guarantees that there will be some surprises for everyone. Among the revelations for me is the Japanese designer Toru Mitani, whose projects include the park and gardens at the Wind Hill Crematory in Nakatsu, in association with buildings by architect Fumihiko Maki. The project is especially intriguing, a shallow dish of space that functions both as a public park and place for private commemoration.

Work also appears here for some unusual contexts, notably a therapeutic garden at a facility for the treatment of severely traumatized children in Wellesley, Massachusetts, begun in the office of Child Associates and completed by Douglas Reed. It consists of a sequence of spaces leading farther and farther from the treatment center, each with its own challenges to physical and emotional resilience. A child's willingness to adventure through the spaces evidently can have both diagnostic and therapeutic implications.

While presenting built work, the Forum ought to be responsive to more theoretical, conceptual, or visionary approaches as well. With nature increasingly under assault from simulated and virtual analogues, we might debate, for example, if the attachment to the exterior, physical environment isn't in danger of becoming nostalgic, and if the most telling conceptions of nature aren't now to be found inside our shopping malls, theme parks, televisions, and computers. A few projects presented here begin to toy with some of these ideas, notably Peter Walker's design for the Kempinski Hotel in Munich, where glass cases containing plastic geraniums are to be found both inside and outside the hotel lobby, blurring the distinctions between exterior and interior, natural and artificial. Otherwise, however, built projects might not be the first place to look for evidence of the evolving culture of nature.

All this suggests that the designed landscape is not one phenomenon but several, and that it is perceived differently by the various professions. For sculptors, the landscape has become a way of escaping the narrow formalist concerns that came to dominate art in the Modernist era, a means of infusing the static, portable, indoor esthetic object with real-life temporal, topographic, and social characteristics. For designers, however, the physical and social features of the landscape are familiar territory, and many of them seem determined to enhance the artistic dimensions of their practice. Planners might be surprised to hear that their work lacks sufficient evidence of self-conscious artistry to register as design, while preservationists might be excused for finding all the emphasis on esthetics very much beside the point, as field and forest, not to mention historically significant and diverse human and biotic communities, are swallowed up in featureless sprawl. Suffice it to say that the precise dimensions and character of the designed landscape are a matter for further explication.

The parochial schism between what I might term the pattern makers and the eco-warriors also needs to be resolved. The latter, I think, can fairly complain that they are held to a higher standard than the former. Ecology-driven projects are typically assessed on their design merits, while the more formal interventions are not always judged in ecological terms. Bill Wenk Associates' Shop Creek Stream Restoration in Aurora, Colorado, for example, is generally lauded for the elegance with which it resolves problems of erosion, recreating a self-sustaining ecology through the use of crescent-shaped soil-cement berms that appear to nest in the existing stream bed. But it is faulted for having no obvious circulation pattern for human users and little visible connection to the larger cultural context. Meanwhile, dozens of form-driven projects escape evaluation on their ecological merits. It might be interesting to devise a "sustainability index" that would measure such factors as resource consumption, irrigation and maintenance needs, and habitat formation, and apply it to projects like Peter Walker's South Coast Plaza Town Center in Costa Mesa or Mark Rios' private garden in Los Angeles, to see how they stack up against more assertively ecological works.

The point to be grasped, I think, is that a systemic view of landscape demands that formal, ecological, historical, and social concerns must be layered in every project. There is some evidence in the works examined here that this is beginning to occur. Exemplary in this regard is Mario Schjetnan's Xochimilco Natural Park in Mexico City, part of a larger project to restore some 3,000 hectares of ancient lacustrine environment in the Valley of Mexico. Listed as one of UNESCO's world heritage sites in 1987, the Xochimilco area includes numerous canals and lagoons as well as "floating islands" that have been in agricultural use since Precolonial times. In addition to cleaning and dredging the canals, restoring the water quality, and reclaiming the floating islands, the project includes a 270-hectare park designed by Schjetnan. The park encompasses recreational, historic, educational, and working landscapes; it includes a flower market, a reproduction of the artificial agricultural islands, active and passive relaxation areas, and ethnographic, botanic, and archeological exhibits.

Other projects suggest the same blend of formal and ecological ambitions. Lorna Jordan's Waterworks Gardens, a stormwater treatment project in Renton, Washington, designed in conjunction with Jones and Jones of Seattle, collects runoff in leaf-shaped ponds where sediment and contaminants are allowed to settle out. The design includes several intriguing sculptural elements, notably a mosaic-encrusted, hosed-concrete grotto through which cleansed water cascades.

Resolving these parochial matters would enable designers to move on to other questions with profound implications for the character of the built landscape: whether bigness has to equal banality;

whether a theory-driven practice is possible; and whether regionalism is still viable in a global marketplace. As firms grow, will the quality of their work inevitably diminish? With more of them practicing overseas, will they be attentive to local cultures, or will an insensitive one-style-suits-all approach become the norm? Does there exist a significant body of critical and theoretical writing within the landscape professions, or is theory thus far merely an overlay from other disciplines? Can we imagine a theory with truly practical applications and a practice with a theoretical basis of real substance?

There are many other urgent matters to address. Few developer-driven projects are in evidence here, yet they represent one of the most problematic aspects of contemporary design. Nature seems increasingly vestigial in proliferating commercial spaces— megamalls and urban entertainment districts such as Universal City Walk in Los Angeles or Canal Center Hakata in Fukuoka, Japan. Intensive use and gaudy architectural context add up to an environment that is indifferent if not hostile to landscape.

Landscape designers also need to become more visible in infrastructure projects; few are presented here, other than Royston Hanamoto Alley & Abey's water filtration plant in San Francisco, which has ignited some debate because it is mostly tucked away below. What other kinds of infrastructure projects might be imagined? How can we advance the restoration of degraded urban and industrial landscapes? Most renewal projects opt for amelioration, but what might we do besides creating pleasant spaces out of blight? Shall we try urban agriculture? Can we imagine a design that might address systemic problems of resource consumption and waste, illuminating the social processes that led to disruption in the first place?

As in psychoanalysis, what might be most revealing about this book is not what is spoken but what is omitted. What should be of concern is what we are not seeing as much as what is presented. Where are the landscapes of the highway, the mall, the theme park, and the parking lot? How shall we come to terms with the terrains of commerce and entertainment? Landscape design seems frighteningly irrelevant to much of what gets built. Perhaps designers and artists ought to be more proactive, seeking opportunities instead of waiting for them to be presented. Rather than letting patronage alone determine where and how the landscape professions are practiced, designers could insert themselves into the contexts where significant development is taking place and become a guiding force.

Above all, everyone concerned with the landscape needs to continue the project of reimagining it in terms of interlocking cultural and natural systems, addressing landscape not as a static, passive ground but as a dynamic space in the process of transformation. In this initial venture, the Designed Landscape Forum takes the character of a report on where the professions have been in the past decade. And it raises questions that should guide their development in the years to come.

On behalf of the Designed Land-scape Forum Board of Directors and the Conference and Publication Committees, I would like to thank all those who gave their time and financial support to make the Designed Landscape Forum such a rewarding success. Thanks also to those who submitted entries, to the panelists, and the conference participants. The Forum is a labor of love and contribution. The many telephone calls, faxes, and notes of encouragement and congratula-tions are deeply appreciated.

The initial response to the Designed Landscape Forum has been truly overwhelming and extremely positive from both the attending press and the profes-sional participants. A book encom-passing the first entries, to be published this Fall, will enable a considerably wider review by those artists, architects, urban designers, landscape architects, photogra-phers, environmental graphic designers, and others interested in the built outdoor environment.

The majority of the 250 submissions were of built work showing a wide variety of specific approaches and points of view. This, the Board and conference participants feel, pro-vides an interesting snapshot of the state of the art of landscape design at this moment in time. The Board intends to repeat the conference in November 1998 on the East Coast.

But what of the theoretical and visionary aspects of the designed landscape? The plans, the models for future projects, and specula-tions for the future? To explore these questions, the DLF Board of Directors is proposing a call for unbuilt landscape designs to be published by Spacemaker Press in 1998.

We hope to hear from many of you, and to seeing you in 1998 at the next Designed Landscape Forum.
—Cheryl Barton

the unbuilt landscape
call for entries

Call for entries: From Artists, Landscape Architects, Architects, Urban Designers, Graphic Designers, and Photographers of the designed landscape. The **Second Annual Designed Landscape Forum** is seeking entries for **Unbuilt Landscapes**. The entries may range from proposals for future construction through regional, subregional, or site-specific plans, to visionary speculations. Entries may range from art to ecologically determined proposals, from abstract dreams to political document. **Deadline for submissions is January 15, 1998.** Entries selected by the judges will be included in a book to be published by Spacemaker Press. **What to submit: 1.** One PMT or photo print of the plan and/or sections and elevations (preferably black-and-white line drawings). **2.** Ten reproduction-quality 35mm slides numbered with captions and photo credits. **3.** One page with name of project, designers and/or design firm, project location, size, date, principle design concept, and description of project in not more than 500 words. **4.** A disk with all text, including captions and credits. **5.** $75 entry fee per project. $50 for students with a valid ID. Payable by check. More than one project submission is allowed and encouraged. **Send all entries to:** Designed Landscape Forum, 147 Sherman Street, Cambridge, MA 02140, by January 15, 1998. Entries will not be returned. By entering this competition, the entrant grants the Designed Landscape Forum and Spacemaker Press permission to publish the material entered, and to use the material for promotional purposes associated with the book, with Spacemaker Press, and the Designed Landscape Forum. Credit will be given for all uses of the material.

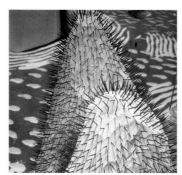

"Island Culture" by Wellington Reiter, Cambridge Massachusetts

The Unbuilt Landscape Call For Entries: (duplicate as necessary). This form must accompany your entries.

Name _____ Firm or School:_____

Address _____

City _____ State_____ ZIP_____

Phone _____ Fax_____ E-mail_____ www_____

Number of Entries @ US $75 (students with copy of ID @ $50):_____ Total amount of check:_____

I understand the terms of this submission. You have my permission to publish all materials.

I will take responsibility to get releases from clients and photographers. All items **1, 2, 3, 4, 5** are enclosed.

Signed _____ Date _____